Bonesetter Gerry O'Donoghue at work

For Donald

"*This book opens a door into the Burren as a place of wellbeing and welcomes you in. Here you will read stories, in their own words, of local farmers, herbalists, doctors, faith healers, bone-setters and others. Their dialogue has been minimally edited, allowing their personalities to shine through.*"

Dr Eamon Doyle *-Geologist*

"*A terrific compendium of Burren people and what makes them tick as well as being a really interesting and worthwhile addition to the rich corpus of literary material produced by Burren people in recent years.*"

Gordon D'Arcy
- Artist and author of 'The Breathing Burren'

3

First published 2019 by Newheart Health Publications, Co. Clare

Photographs by **Eamon Ward** and Eilís Haden-Storrie

Layout and Design by Paul Dunne, Rock Rose Creations

ACKNOWLEDGEMENTS

Thank you to all of you who gave up your time in support of this project. Through your comments, feedback and inspiration you have been part of a growing and continuing movement towards understanding and cohesion between nature, healers, health professionals and all of us who wish to be well. Thanks in particular to Jenny Lambert, Dympna Keenan, Ruairí Ó'Conchúir, Gerry (Hoppy) and Ciara O'Haloran, Clare Sheehan, Bríd Keely, Colin Dempsey and Kelly Johnson for sharing your personal experiences and knowledge. Thanks to Jackie Fahy, The Bishop's Quarter Bathers and The Ballyvaughan & Fanore Walking Club for your listening ear, friendships and laughter on the mountains and in the sea. Thank you, Kathleen Lynn, Elenore Quigly and the Flaggy Shore merpeople for being trail blazers and to Ciara Russell and all of the swimmers at Trácht for the beautiful full-moon swim experiences. Thanks to Brother Colmán Ó Clabaigh for the advice and references and to Fathers Brian and Christopher from Glenstal Abbey for creating a sanctuary of peace in which to spend the long days drafting and re-drafting. Thanks to Padraic for the push and to Ger Ryan, Deirdre

Ruane and everyone at The Burren Enterprise Centre for their company and laughter during the time spent editing this book. Thanks to John O'Neill for enhancing my love of words. Thanks to Rupert Bagwell for the gift of Qi Gong, Geraldine Linnane for the constructive feedback, and Maria Kerin, Mary Glynn and Fran Brady for their warmth, wisdom and continuous encouragement. Thanks to Joan O'Loughlin for the loan of the books, Peadar Kelly and Patsy Mullins for sharing their knowledge of agriculture and fishing. Thanks to Creative Ireland, Dr. Eamon Doyle and all at the Geopark office for their generous support the overall project of which this book is one part. Thanks to Kinvara FM and all media bodies who have promoted this book. Thanks to Paddy Dunne at Lisdoonvarna Fáilte and his team for the introduction to their work with the Sulphur Wells, thanks to my family including Mary Burke, wider circle of friends and anyone who deserves gratitude but who has momentarily slipped from memory. Thanks to the Hansard team with whom I learned to improve my grammar, Brendan Hokowhitu and Te Ruru for opening my eyes and finally, to those who gave a smile or kind word in passing over the course of the past year; your name may not have been mentioned but your energy is imprinted in this project.

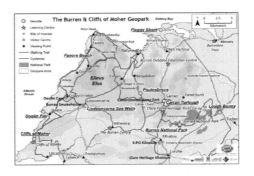

FORWARD

In the 1930s the Irish Folklore Commission carried out a survey of Irish folk practices. For this, primary school students across the country were asked to interview the older people in their community about traditional beliefs. County Clare, and in particular the Burren, was found to have a large density of folk cures and practicing healers. You might say this was due to the magic and energy of the place or purely to the simplicity of life in small farming villages where money was short and general practitioners were scarce. Or, we could see it as a combination of both. Either way, it highlighted that the old traditions were alive and well and local people were reaping the benefits.

Talking with the many farmers, healers and practitioners who kindly gave up their time for this research I was struck by how many hold the belief that most of what they do is simply to enable nature to nurture us. Whether this is done through tinctures, tablets and tree poses, through the release of negative energy, the creation of safe place where we feel accepted and heard and, in cases where there's no cure, through the facilitation of acceptance and grace is up for grabs. But the overarching sense seems to be that having strong resources of healing to draw on all around us is a huge comfort and privilege.

All these profiles are of people who have studied, carry out their healing practices and/or live in the Burren, Co. Clare, a 250 km² UNESCO-protected conservation area, home to 18 villages and towns. The interviews have been recorded as part of an eleven-month collaborative process whereby participants can examine their initial transcript and adapt it so as to tell their story as fully as possible. In addition, most are given in verbatim form so you can get a true sense of the personality of each contributor.

My Masters Degree is in Indigenous Studies via the Department of Māori and Pacifica Studies in Otago, Aotearoa/New Zealand. Kaupapa Māori research methods dictate that we must clearly state our place in

Eileen & Melissa Jeunken

any given piece of research. So here it is; For decades I burned my feet in the race to beat the black dog. Looking back, I think it first appeared during early-childhood bouts of glandular fever but eventually I created my own dramas and soon the dog lurking behind every corner. That running lead me into being a risk taker to the extreme and life became a pendulum of exhilaration, cataclysmic successes and failures and, in the months where it caught up, immobilising darkness. This journey meandered from an international private boarding school to a flat off Dublin's Sherriff Street with no heating or plaster on the walls, months of surviving on Vincent de Paul food vouchers, followed by years of research into sectarian violence in Northern Ireland, a stint as a human-rights observer in Hebron and endless lone meanderings where I sat in corners and witnessed life's brilliance and madness in full technicolor. But this race never lead me to a place of self-care or compassion. Eventually I landed at a precipice where the only options were to jump or learn how to live. I jumped and there's no scientific explanation as to the survival that followed. What might only be described as a miracle led to the slow backward-forward process of recovery. Self-harm and anorexia can be like the itch you can't scratch;

but once we accept these ailments, learn to manage them and build on our strengths then eventually we can catch glimpses of real joy, self-care and deep-rooted, genuine compassion for others.

Returning to the Burren where I spent 7 years of my childhood had its challenges; things, long ignored had to be faced but without doubt this process has brought real benefit. Many say this is a healing place or thin space and others that this is too romantic a view. But it's easy to accept the healing powers of the sea on the nape of your neck as you do the dolphin kick in Galway bay, or the view of the three ancient churches from the holy well at Uchtmáma, or the bracing salt-filled air as you cycle along the coast road with its sheer drop down into the ocean. These are things that can fill us with awe and simple joy. Nature will offer itself to us as mother and healer; all we have to do is connect.

That said, self-care and recovery will only come after we've learned to like ourselves. We live in a world of comparisons, where we often feel we don't measure up and so it can be a challenge to feel we deserve to spend time and money on our wellbeing. We get into the habit of eating sugar every time it's offered, buying veg that's been pesticide-sprayed to within an inch of its life and watching TV shows that numb our brains. Perhaps the only time we felt truly nurtured, as children, was when we were sick and so we manifest this need in older age or loneliness by seeking out the listening ear or kind touch of a health practitioner. There are so many reasons why we have yet to evolve in terms of maintaining wellness but the emergence of social prescribing and integrated health care show we're headed in a positive direction.

In a world where medical and alternative practitioners are baffled by the issue of patient compliance – where people know what they need so as to manage their health but continue with behaviours that are detrimental - I hope this book will shine a little light. So, if you care about your own healing and wellness and if you value mental, spiritual and physical nourishment then this book is for you. If you love Ireland and the unique Burren conservation area and want to learn more about how the land and sea nurture us and how we can sustain and show gratitude for this energy, then this is the book for you. If you enjoy seeing life at its core through the eyes of strong characters, unafraid to live according to their true purpose and fulfil their human and spiritual potential then this is the book for you.

We wish you well and hope you gain as much joy and nourishment from reading this book as came from its creation.

TABLE OF CONTENTS

ACKNOWLEDGEMENTS...5

FORWARD...7

TIMELINE...12

GENERAL INTRODUCTION...20

CHAPTER 1

THE LORE OF FOLK...23

CHAPTER 2

WELLS WHICH MAKE US WELL..68

CHAPTER 3

BEYOND THE SOUL..96

CHAPTER 4

BETWEEN SKY, LAND & SEA...122

CHAPTER 5

FROM THE OUTSIDE IN...154

CONCLUSION..183

BIOGRAPHIES...185

BIBLIOGRAPHY..187

TIMELINE

Events which influenced where we are today

You may find this timeline useful in that it looks at the progression of how we have nurtured ourselves locally, nationally and globally from the earliest stages in our know existence. It has been extensively researched and is a result of the patience of the many academics and environmentalists who kindly gave up their time and blazed these trails before me.

300 million years ago
The Burren karst landscape made up of fossil corals, crinoids and brachiopods is formed in warm tropical sea near the equator

12,500 years ago
Evidence of first humans in Ireland near Ennis, Co. Clare (approx. 13km from the Burren)

4,000BC
Start of Neolithic Period - Hunter gatherers arrive in Fanore

3200BC

Newgrange built; earth mound venerating earth goddess built before pyramids or Stonehenge. Sealed up several hundred years later

3000BC.
Neolithic Period - Early farmers saw the earth and the sky as divine as they took nourishment from that which grew in the earth under the heat of the sun. Evidence of communal burial grounds from this time

2500BC.
Start of Bronze Age - Introduction of copper and bronze working.

More emphasis on individual burial

2200BC.

Near collision of comet into earth with enormous explosion and fire-
balls from sky which scorched parts of the earth. Birth of legend of
Lugh a deity of the skies, similar in form to a comet. Possible lessening
in worship of earth

600BC.

Sushruta, an Indian surgeon performs what is possibly the first recorded
surgical operation – a nose reconstruction - and writes 'Sushruta Sam-
hita' which describes over 300 surgical procedures in meticulous and
comprehensive detail

600BC

End of Bronze Age and beginning of Iron Age

460BC

Hippocrates born - Greek physician known as Father of Western Medicine. Hippocrates is credited as being the first person to believe diseases
are caused naturally and not by the Gods. He also believed all
disease starts in the gut and in the power of nature and the body's ability
to heal itself

432AD

St Patrick arrives in Ireland for purposes of converting its peoples to
Christianity. It's believed that when the lands in Wicklow he is repelled
and has to sail further north to Strangford Lough. The Annals of Ulster
suggest he remained in the north where he only converted 12,000

533-540AD

Huge dust cloud made up of debris from Halley's Comet lingers in
Northern Hemisphere. The Irish Annals from 536-537AD report on
darkness and food shortages

541AD

One third of Europe's population is killed by plague - gradual shift during this century from Druidism to Christianity as perhaps people believe sky Gods have failed them and new religion holds the answers

795AD
First Viking raids on Ireland

1054AD
Division between Eastern Orthodox churches, seen as more mystical, and Catholic church seen as more pragmatic

1155AD
Pope Adrian IV issued papal bull supposedly allowing for King Henry II to occupy Ireland and assist in the reform of the Irish church and system of governance

1184AD
Beginning of medieval inquisition lead by Pope Lucius III to combat public heresy - this series of inquisitions continued until the 1800s

1540AD
English barbers and surgeons unite to form The United Barber-Surgeons Company specialising in bloodletting and tooth extraction. They are a separate group from physicians

1586AD
Plantation of Munster - first mass occupation of Ireland by English crown

1620AD
Visible shift from reasoning (stemming from Aristotle's dependence on the senses) to empiricism (evidence-based conclusions) when Francis Bacon argues for the reestablishment of the "empire of man over creation" lost by the fall in the Garden of Eden. Bacon believed his form of intellectual reasoning would bring an end to poverty and misery

1633AD
Galileo is put under house arrest for the rest of his lifetime for per-

forming act of heresy in stating that earth revolves around the sun

1653AD

Nicholas Culpeper, pharmacist, herbalist and astrologer published 'The Complete Herbal.' Culpeper offered free healing to London's poor and translated medical books into English so that we could learn to heal ourselves

1660AD

Beginning of Penal Law period in Ireland where Catholics and dissenting Protestants such as Presbyterians were prevented from voting, holding public office, owning land and teaching

1711AD

First Irish medical school set up in Trinity College, Dublin

1745AD

The Rotunda Hospital - first charitable maternity hospital in Ireland opened as result of public donations

1838AD

Poor Law Act for the "more effectual relief of the destitute poor" was introduced in Ireland. This resulted in the introduction of infirmaries, dispensaries and medical officers to care for the poor. Reports cite standards as being set intentionally low

1840AD

Trinity College Herbarium, curated by William Henry Harvey, son of a Limerick Quaker is set up. The herbarium identifies plants worldwide and their uses both medical and otherwise

1843AD

1st hysterectomy performed in England

1845AD

The Great Hunger - Period of famine in Ireland - 1 million died and 1 million emigrated

1904AD
Board of Trinity College agrees to the admission of women to study medicine

1918AD
Post WWI Influenza pandemic kills an estimated 50 million people and infects at least one in five globally. 20,057 deaths officially recorded in Ireland. Initially influenza mistakenly thought to be caused by bacteria and not virus

1921AD
Anglo Irish Treaty signed leading to independence of 26 counties from United Kingdom. Catholic church's power increases as it owns hospitals and schools. Church is seen to have animosity towards faith and traditional healers

1928AD
Antibiotics discovered

1937AD
Beginning of Irish Folklore Commission study where 50,000 children in 5,000 schools around Ireland are asked to interview parents, grandparents and neighbours about local folklore including cures and traditional medicines. Large concentration of faith healers and cures found in the Burren

1945AD
End of WW2 brought about largest population movement in European history

1949AD
Government proposes system of universal social insurance which would have set Ireland on course as a welfare state with a universal national health service. This is shelved due to intense opposition from the medical profession, Catholic Church and Department of Finance. The pattern of two-tier health service is established

1955AD

Bord Fáilte Eireann is set up leading to a tourism boom in the 1960s and providing jobs in rural areas

1957AD

VHI - the state-sponsored health insurance scheme set up

1957AD

Heinrich Böll publishes 'Irisches Tagebuch' seen by many as the inspiration behind the huge influx of German immigrants to Ireland. Germans and other post-war immigrants bring new ideas about healthcare, spirituality, conservation, diet and farming methods

1970AD

The medical card system is introduced. System whereby public health services delivered by local government and funded through lotteries such as hospital sweepstakes dies out

1973AD

We join European Economic Community which leads to the gradual introduction of new regulations around food production, farming and medicines

1978AD

First 'test tube' baby (conceived by in vitro fertilization) born in England. First baby born in Ireland through IVF less than a decade later

Circ1980AD

Health Stores promoting alternative practices begin to emerge in Ireland

1986AD

Irish Association of Health Stores set up

1995AD

'Contemporary Health Practices in the Burren' an academic study by Anne Murphy (McFarlane) and Cecily Kelleher, NUIG, examining attitudes towards folk, conventional and alternative medicine in the Burren was published

Mid-1990s

Birth of Celtic Tiger; a period of rapid economic growth fuelled by
foreign direct investment

1997AD

Burren native John Donoghue publishes 'Anam Cara' a bestseller reflecting
on our pre-Christian past and idea of the body as an anchor for the soul

2001AD

Strategy for Control of Antimicrobial Resistance in Ireland launched
advising promotion of prudent use of antibiotics

2005AD

In line with a recommendation of the National Working Group the
Irish government supports greater voluntary self-regulation of the complementary therapy sector

2008AD

End of Celtic Tiger. Ireland plunged into global recession

2008AD

Opening of Steiner school in Ennistymon which is reported to have
attracted many families with more alternative lifestyles to the area

2010AD

Irish Medical Organisation warns the Oireachtas Committee that
thousands of patients are being denied medical card entitlements due to
administrative chaos at the HSE

2013AD

Survey carried out on behalf of the Irish Pharmacy Union found that 1
in 20 patients did not take their medication due to fear of side effects

2017AD

Burren-based American herbalist Tonja Reichtly publishes 'Wild Irish
Roots' in which she highlights cures from our pre-Christian origins

2017AD

Amy Smith of Du Pont highlights potential for takeover in probiotics manufacture by pharma industry. Up to this, probiotics are generally used as dietary supplements where they can be manufactured according to dietary supplement GMPs.

Holy Well, Uchtmáma

GENERAL INTRODUCTION

Imagine Ireland in the middle ages. A motley crew of the fanatical, fervent, pious and placid make their way beside their beasts along grassy and stony paths. They wear coarse, un-dyed robes in the form of tunics to which are attached scapular and hood, some perhaps with lice-infested hair-skin under garments used by monks in those times as a form of penance. Their mission is to seek out a particular shallow fertile valley in an isolated karst landscape and cultivate a monastic haven dedicated to the Virgin Mary.

Their destination is Corcomroe, a spot just over the hill flanked on one side by Kilmacduagh, a 6th Century hermitage site in what became known as the Barony of the Burren and the on the other by a small inlet, home to the Poldoody and Redbank oyster beds; a source of food in those days for the common man, later to fall under the ownership of English kings.

This is a time of great unrest; chief against chief driving whole tribes against one another in bloody battle has been replaced by the no-less-violent Norman invasion. With them these medieval monks bring a heavyweight of sacred texts, vellum and ink for copying and what may have been seedlings of the medicinal plants that they will depend on for their corporal survival through bleak winters and summers of gruelling labour setting up the farm which will feed them for years to come.

In these times the large stone abbeys which replace simpler wooden structures are a new feature of the Irish landscape. But Corcomroe contains what, to this day, is a rarity in the form of carvings of medicinal herbs and plants around what must have been the most prominent building in its grounds; the presbytery. If you look closely you'll see images in its capitals of what look like the opium poppy, used for rheumatism, nervous afflictions and pain, Solomon's seal used for broken bones, wounds and bruises, Lilly of the Valley used for heart trouble and, for what reasons we can only guess, deadly nightshade which could kill a child with just three berries. As to why the monks chose to feature these plants be it for the sake of aesthetics or a reverence for the only forms of medicines this isolated community had access to, we'll never know.

PJ Curtis, who features in this book, talks about cures using plant names in Old Latin that have been handed down through his family for generations. He muses that these may have come from the monks of Corcomroe as they were the only locals using Old Latin and, it's well known that many herbs and cures were introduced to Ireland through the church via the Greeks and Romans.

And so we learn that these monks who came to Corcomroe in the 1200's brought with them flowers from around Europe;

they grew them from seed, nurtured and protected them. These were the plants which were to keep the monks well and healthy. And then, it might appear, these cures were passed on to nearby families like the Curtises who used them on local people for centuries to come.

We can only imagine how this isolated religious community would have revered these cures as a means to sustain their earthly bodies. But do we revere modern medicines now? These days, we don't see how our cures are made; we don't see the plants in the ground, we don't grow or nurture them – they're made in some factory a long way away through an invisible process. We just go to a doctor and they hand us a prescription for what seems like an endless supply. The process is invisible and, as far as we can see, doesn't even come from nature.

We imagine how conscientious the monks would have been about keeping these curative plants safe. A storm or virus that decimated their herbal crop might have led to great suffering the next time there was an illness or emergency. So, where are we going with modern medicine? How have we come from this isolated 12th Century Irish abbey, a place where medicine was revered to a time when many of us just want to see a doctor and pop a pill thus giving away our power. And how do we get back to a place where nature is nurtured by us and we, in turn, are nurtured by nature.

Holy Well, Uchtmáma

CHAPTER 1
THE LORE OF FOLK

Faith, Flowers & Bone Setters

Studies by the Smithsonian Institute suggest that the early Celts worshipped the gods of the earth. This is easy to understand given the newness of farming and the abundance it provided. But in 2200 BC we're told that a comet nearly collided with our home planet causing huge explosions which scorched much of the land. Crops failed and the earth dried up resulting in widespread famine. The legend of Lugh, a deity of the skies who was shaped like a comet, may have arisen as a result of this and so, it's believed, our focus of worship shifted from that which is below to that which is above. This research from the Smithsonian Institute maintains that on his arrival, St Patrick and the ideas of Christianity were met with little enthusiasm until the onset of a subsequent famine caused by dust clouds made up of debris from Halley's Comet which lingered for seven years. And so it's put to us that, whether through a sense of damnation or inefficacy of their beliefs, the Irish shifted their allegiances to a system that worshiped one god in whose image man was made. It's interesting to speculate, that if this is so then perhaps it was the beginning of the time when we started to shift from honouring the earth and the sky to seeing mankind as a reflection of the true source of power. Of course, this is up for debate, but we cannot question that in today's world where 55% of the population live in cities, we've disconnected from nature in its rawest form and many of our children have never even seen a plant grow.

According to Allen and Hatfield, mass migration to towns and cities began when land enclosures of the 17th century led to the gradual demise of the common ownership system. Two-and-a-half centuries later, over a million people emigrated from Ireland to America during the great famine and whole villages in the Burren disappeared. As a result of this, many folk traditions across the British Isles were lost.

But some did survive and DNA tests on local school children have shown that a few families currently farming the Burren have been here since the bronze age which started 2,500 years ago. These families have carried local knowledge of the importance of nature and its healing properties from its conception through to today. These are families who witnessed the evolution of the healing arts in the Burren and a more-recent falloff in the numbers of faith healers and bone setters. One of the few remaining bone setters in the whole of Ireland now lives in Gort where he treats horses, dogs and humans from as far away as Cork and Donegal with some Irish coming home from America and England for the cure.

Gerry O'Donoghue
Bone setter from Gort

I love where I came from. My family came from Kerry originally, they were drovers who ended up in Boston, Co. Clare sometime in the '40s. My father got a thatched house that my brother still lives in. My mother had eleven children, the oldest and the youngest died. She died when she was about fifty-two. She was a young woman. She fed the parish. My father was a great character. He did all the castrating and killing of pigs and all those kinds of jobs around the area - he was a mighty man to survive. He reared all of us on 21 acres. We were never hungry or short of anything. We may have been poor, but we didn't know we were poor. I went butchering in 1979. I served my apprenticeship in Ennis and then opened the shop in Gort in 1986 and I'm here ever since. We have three young lads and three girls; they're mad for hurling, mad for greyhounds, they love life and they're as happy as Larry. They're well able to fight and argue and that's my life story.

A bone setter is an unqualified man who can realign bones in a person's body. He has no qualifications, he cannot write it down, he can't give you the cert to say he did this or did that but 'tis a natural gift and you don't even know how you do it. There was one in every parish one time, going back in the '30s, cos there was no transport. People couldn't travel so there was a healer or bone setter in every parish. But it died out with modern technology. It died out with the scans. Qualified chiropractors and all that came into play and they learned it out of a book.

Normally it would be passed down through the family; from father to son. T'would be like with a sheepdog; the mother would teach the son how to work.

You had a lot of women who were into the herbs - curing with herbs and all that. The most famous one was Biddy Early; she was a great healer. But unfortunately, the clergy didn't like her and gave her a bad name just to bring her down a step or two. There's all different styles of bone setters. In my style of bone setting, I divine the body. So when a person comes into me for a healing session, or whatever, I don't even ask them what's up; we divine the body itself - we go through the whole body. And with the divining, we can find if a bone is out of place. Like you hear people saying, "He has a disk out in his back." But that doesn't happen; they are trapped together, and we are able to find the ones that are trapped and release them - take the pressure off it. But if it's a person with a bone in their finger or their ankle, you can just pop it into place.

With divining you can use different materials; I use a coat hanger. Some people use a sally rod or whatever. Some people divine for water or divine for electricity; I divine bad energy or blockages in the body - bones out of place - simple as that. We will go down along a person's spine. When we hit a spot the wire just goes 'Bang! There you are!!' We have a certain way that we use everybody; we start from the top of their head down to their spine, out to their pelvis, back up their shoulders and down along their legs.

We go through the same rituals with everybody and find the blockages if they're there. Because your body is full of electricity and water; they have to flow and if the energy is not flowing properly in your body you are going to pay - you're going to be in trouble. What we do is like taking a stone out of the river and letting off the water.

Spine Healing

There's no science to it, it's just a thing that works. Some people get fantastic results, some people say "Jaysus, it was a load of shite; it didn't work for me." For some people it mightn't be their man d'you know, it mightn't be... they could be unwell, they could have other diseases, there could be things wrong with them; their blood could be ruined with arthritis or whatever or your work might just not be good enough for them. That's unfortunate but if you got them earlier when the rot started in, if you got in first, you might have been able to reverse it, or whatever. But if they were gone too long... Like sometimes a person's back would be gone so bad you wouldn't be able to fix it. You could put it back into line but by the time they were back out in the car it would be gone again so you wouldn't succeed all the time.

I'm 30 years doing this. I've often done a person and it never went wrong again, and then I'd see a person every three years or three weeks in a row; you just mightn't get it in one go. But when people ask, "Can I come back?" I say, "No. I'm like the A.I. man; I don't want to see you back. I don't need to see you again because, to me, that would mean I didn't do my job properly the first day and I haven't time to be seeing people two or three times. I want to get the job done once and get a success." And also, it's to do with a person's mind; a lot of people are so accustomed to going back to places after two weeks… To me, if it doesn't work it doesn't work. I don't do this for a living, so I want to get a success with a person and move on and fix the next one if I'm able. For people with back problems, it's not that they're holding the body wrong. The brain tricks the body; it moves the body away from pain. So, you'd often see someone with a vertebra trapped in his back - he'd be gone to one side and it would go down his leg but that's the brain tricking the body. The brain is trying to trick the body to an ease that he would be comfortable with, so when you release the pressure that body should come back to normal; like, when the energy is right.

We have six kids and so there's always roaring and shouting in this house. But not only kids; I came back here last Sunday and there was women sleeping all over the place. Anybody who would be stuck in town would sleep here; friends of the young lads and that. It's kind of like a cúirting house similar to what we had at home. There are very few houses in Gort that you go to visit now. In our house anyone could call into it; make the tea for themselves and whatever. It's probably the way we were raised at home; we knew no better. But now since they got the few pound people put on the 'f**k-off' gates as I call it.

I don't know where the tradition of faith healing came from, but I always felt that… if I saw a person walking 'round I'd say, "He's walking wrong". It was always kind of there and I don't even know how I started it, or why I started it or how it led to what it is today. Like, if someone came into the shop and they had a pain in their face or eyes, I could see something in them. Though I never imagined for one minute or one second that there would be people coming back from England and America to get help. And like, there just now in the shop I got a phone call from a woman in Donegal. That's mad like, d'you know.

Everybody you work on teaches you to the next person and then you can remember what you saw before. The modern practitioners don't want to look on what was before; they go round in a circle and do all the tests. We don't go round in circles, we go straight through it, d'you know what I mean. We'd have seen it before and there's no rocket science; it's straightforward - if the wheel is punctured it's punctured. Some people you wouldn't be able to help but you'd know someone that would. So, like, somebody might need to go to a chiropractor or acupuncturist or a homeopath, or it could be a person's diet or something. And through the years of working with people and seeing the mistakes they are making, and mistakes you made from your own life as well, you would learn from that and you would be able to put them on the right road.

Apart from bone alignment a lot of illness is caused by people's diet; eating crap and it's not suiting their blood. Like I would say, petrol car - put in petrol, diesel car - put in diesel. I also follow a book that an American professor wrote called 'Live Right for your Type'. I'd advise people to buy that book and read it. It is about living for your blood type. The reason a lot of Irish people got riddled with arthritis and their hips got rotten is because they all ate the pig. And 90% of Irish people are O positive or O negative right?! And the pig is damn nearly the same gene or blood type. And because the pig is cheap they ate it - they could afford nothing else and so they were eating themselves. And that is why you saw a lot of people when I was a young fella going around with sticks; 'cos the hips were rotten off them. So, if you are O positive you shouldn't eat pig. It's a great auld book, you should read it.

People put names on us, but I don't describe myself as anything. I don't describe myself as doing this work at all. I believe somebody else does the work 'cos how could I know how to align a person's body or how could I know how to put a dog's back right or a person's back right or put in a shoulder with no qualifications so obviously there is somebody else helping me do that cos I am an ordinary fellow; Gerry Donoghue who lives in Gort, he's a butcher. It is sort of contradictory so there is something else there. I don't know what it is. I always say,

"We will be working tomorrow" because if I thought for one minute that it was I that was doing this work, I'd go wrong in the head, d'you know what I mean. You see there is something else and whether somebody chose me to do this work or not - because I didn't choose to do this work; I never went out looking, I never advertised, and I'd never say to a person "You are wrong there" or whatever. 'Cos if you did say that to a person they'd say "Aww no! I'd never f*?*ing believe in that" or whatever so I would never put myself forward or anything. But we can see the results we can get with the animals; like the results we get with the greyhounds. We did the derby winner this year; we did him every Sunday morning. His trainer is a very quiet unassuming man and would be very, very well got say with the vets, and he chooses to use our work every week because he can see the results we get. The divining is

Animal Divining

the same with the dog; we go through his muscles and his tendons. If there's an injury there in his body we will be able to find it.

A greyhound is all about time. Let's say a greyhound is able to do the race in 20 seconds but if he loses his form he goes back to doing it in 30 seconds. By looking at him physically the ordinary naked eye can see nothing wrong with him. He has no broken bones, there is nothing hanging off but when we divine him we find that his back is outa line and his pelvis is outa line. We pull him back straight, put his energy back straight, say "Give him 10 days off." And he'll come back and do 29 seconds. So that's as near to science as what I can bring to what I do.

Vets are different. I would never compare myself to a vet or anything. He would take his bloods and maybe check tendons and muscles, but he wouldn't be able to find... Like the divining rod is able to find such detail and no matter how good your hands would be you wouldn't be able to find it. Some dogs don't react to pain; like there are pressure points in a dog such as those in its wrists and you would get an odd tough dog that wouldn't react to it, but the divining rod would be able to find it. I didn't know anyone who did divining in our area when I was a kid but early on we used to go to a man in Ballylanders and he used to divine the dogs and divine people. Years back I saw Maurice Lane working at it and we were chatting away because I always had a great interest and at that time I could do injuries in dogs. Then I was talking with another man out the road; Tommy Flannigan the electrician who used to divine and he said to me "Gerry you'd be able to do that." I said, "Jaysus, I would not!" And he said "Why wouldn't you? Shure you're O negative, and all diviners are O negative. Have a go there." So, we started messing about with it. And now we're doing the top racing dogs in Ireland. You know if there's any trouble with a greyhound in Ireland there'd be two or three people you'd go to and we'd be one of them. Like, if you have a top-class dog; one that you want to keep at peak, you would use the divining.

The western medicine, we need it as well; it's important. But the overuse of it is seriously bad; you go into any house and it's full of tablets. The western medicine cured the Tuberculosis, but you have to think why did the people get TB in the first place. There's rakes of things you could question and doubt but I'm not going into conspiracies - everybody can have a conspiracy. Really, it's like we are all drones and they can do what they like with us. But I don't waste my energy thinking about rubbish like that because if you are trying to save the world and sort everybody out then you have no time for yourself and no time to do nothing. So I like to focus my energy on helping a person if I can and not to ever do bad to a person. Once you know the difference between good and bad there is no fear of you, and you are a good human being. I wouldn't be religious at all, I'd be a scarce mass goer enough; Christmas day maybe if I got up, and a funeral and my daughter's wedding or whatever. But I wouldn't be anti-religious either. I believe that if the human body is looked after properly it shouldn't need anything like blood pressure tablets or cholesterol tablets. A good pair of walking boots would cure both of them, d'you know what I mean. And a good healthy diet. Not to be eating pizzas or auld shite; food that's made up for 10 days. I mean our bodies weren't made for that. And shure, every second person is on anxiety tablets, and this new cholesterol thing - they're all on cholesterol tablets. If you're over level 5 - Oh Jaysus you're going to die! Shure it's a load of rubbish. And the red steroids; they're all on them, everybody's on them. Like I say, I'm not knocking the people who are selling them because people are looking for them; they're looking for quick cures, they want to press a button and get better but sometimes that doesn't happen you know.

When I came to Gort there were two doctors here and one chemists. Then the other chemist's opened. At the time, there was about five butchers and supermarkets and shops every place; the whole town was really busy. You now have two butcher shops struggling to survive; both selling the things you most need every day - vegetables and meat. But we have three chemists and the three of them have five or six staff and are massive busy so what the F**k is going wrong? What has happened, what has changed? Why do we need all this medicine? What do we need it for? Does it do any good? That's the question I ask. I'm not anti it now: If a person needs medication, they need medication.

I have two daughters nurses and they are midwives and I agree there's times you need antibiotics and whatever but to me the over sale of drugs is just- you cannot believe it. And all them, every bit of that is being washed down into the water that we have to re-drink; the likes of me who don't take tablets has to re-drink that. So where is it going? It's going into our soil, it's destroying our land. And the slurry the farmers are putting out is destroying all the worms in our land with the gasses; you have no drainage in the land anymore. You go out to dairy farmers' fields now and dig them up and you won't see a worm. When you used to dig up the land at home there would be a million seagulls and birds behind the plough - but you can plough a dairy farm now and there'd be no seagulls or birds because there are no worms; the gasses have them killed. So that's the way our society is going and if it doesn't stop it's not good.

The Burren isn't so bad because you have different soil. In the middle of the Burren they're doing the winterage feeds. They are really on top of that and it's fantastic. This part of the world is going to be saved because someone a good few years ago had the mindset to say, "We've got to protect this area." When the slurry is condensed it turns out to gas and when it's put out on the good land it smothers it and when the worm comes up it's smothered and is dead. With winterage you don't have the slurry. And the cattle are fed properly; there's a different nut specially made for them which is natural so you would have healthier cattle. The majority of cattle in other places are inside in sheds in the winter and if one gets pneumonia they'll all get it and the only way you are going to cure it is through antibiotics but that's for another day - that is not my job.

I think people come to a bone setter as opposed to a doctor 'cos of desperation. We are the last resort. So that's why we have a great success rate; because they've tried everything else and it hasn't worked for them. So, then they say "Well, we'll give this a go." And the person that comes to me has a great chance of getting better 'cos they want to get better. They don't want to be fecked up or unwell. They're hardworking people who need to get going or else they're in trouble.

I work of a Wednesday and last Wednesday morning we had a monitor outside the door that showed people were queuing up at half-seven. We were supposed to start at nine and finish at one o'clock, but I finished at three and all I had was two cups of tea. Now I wouldn't be five minutes with a person unless they needed to talk; like if they were really in a bad f*!%*ing place and they wanted someone to guide them; tell them the truth and try to help them - then you might have to spend longer. But if it was a person whose back would be outa line or who twisted an ankle or something, it would be five minutes in and out - 'Bang! Good luck

Onlookers at Kilbacanty

and bye bye.' We don't delay them or anything alright. So that's a lot of people.

Then we go and do the horses and we would be roughly an hour-and-a-half working on them depending; you could have one horse and you could have ten horses depending on the time of the year. In the winter you would have all hunting horses but in the spring the show jumping horses and the trotters come. Then you'd have the racehorses and show jumpers in the summer and at the back end of the year the hunting horses again. They have come from Donegal, Dublin, and Belfast with the horses. But that's if they are serious about getting a result. They don't come for the fun of it and we don't send for them, so someone must have told them.

If you were to talk to me now you'd know I'm awful easy to talk with and I like to keep a nice banter with people; we'd have the chat and the craic d'you know. And even if a person is really serious, I'd like to get

Gerry's divining rod

them to smile and relax. I'd say to them "Well, you're not at the dentist." Because if a body is tensed up you can't really get to the root of it.

The normal job we're at would be to do with backs or the sciatic nerve with the pain going into their backside and down the leg and we'd be able to fix that.

Some would be nervous of you if they hadn't been here before. They would be chatting with the others waiting outside asking what it's like. If there was a character in the line they might say to a woman something like "Jazus, you've to take off all your clothes!" They have their banter and so the person might be a nervous wreck coming in.

I'll tell you a story. When I was a child and we'd be in Ennis selling the vegetables at the market every Saturday, our father used to get us children to go up to the Poor Clares and leave whatever was left over at the door. I was always reared to see the Poor Clares as real holy people, but I didn't know much about them. Then about maybe 15 years ago one of them was crippled with her back and she came to see me. It was the woman who was doing their garden that brought her. And I was really nervous 'cos I'd be in the habit of f*&%ing and blinding; unfortunately, my tongue isn't great. I was nervous that I'd curse in front of her. And I was doing a job on her backside down to her leg down as far as her ankle; her nerve was trapped. And there was real tension in the room, and I wouldn't like that, I'd like it to be easy you know and chatting and all that, so I said to her, "Tell me sister, were you ever caught on the leg by a man?" and she said "D'you know Gerry, not as hard as that." And this broke the ice. But the woman who was with her said: "Now didn't I tell you what type of a whore he was *[laughs]*?!" So, they're not all holy! That's the kind of craic we have d'you know. That would be our mindset to have a bit of fun. And since then, they've come to visit me three or four times a year. So, I really got to know them. D'you know it's nice; they sent me postcards and that and people give them donations from me. Even though I wouldn't be that religious myself, I'd say "Say a few prayers for me; I wouldn't have time to say them. *[laughs]*" And they'd say they would. Whether they do or not, I dunno but they'd say they would.

My kids don't take much notice of the healing because it's always part of their life. There's people could call at 12 o'clock at night if they were in trouble and for the kids they don't know anything different. They don't even talk about it to their friends because it's just what their father does. One of my girls who's a midwife in England puts a bone out in her back and we have to align her every time she gets home. She just says "Dad, do my back here quick." 'Tis only a two-minute job. It's just part of who we are.

I don't get up in the morning and think about what I do. You go out and do your days' work; it's just part of who you are. You gotta take the good with the bad and hopefully, there is more goods than bads.

You do have bad experiences as well when you wouldn't be able to help someone, and you'd have to say, "I can do nothing for you." Sometimes you'd see something in a person, and you'd know the end story wouldn't be good. The worst part of our job is sometimes a person would come to you and you'd know you could do nothing for them but out of desperation they'd come anyways; they'd try to cling onto something. But I'd be very black and white with that. If there's a family member with them I'd say "Here - I'm not your man' d'you know." Because like I say I don't want people coming back to me 'cos you know… Honesty's the most important thing in our job right but sometimes it's hard to be honest and be nice about being honest because a person might be terminally unwell, and you'd be no good for them. That's the worst part of our job. But the straightforward run of the business, like a person with a bad back or someone with a frozen shoulder, that's straightforward and something our work is able to do.

Unfortunately now, you get an odd person that would be very negative and sees you as - what way will I word it - as an opportunist. And then you doubt yourself and think "F**k! Maybe I shouldn't be doing this at all." And then you meet a person whose back is destroyed, and

Checking a horse's gait

you know you can fix them and so why would you not do it. But sometimes, you would doubt yourself and say you know… "Maybe this is not right what I'm at." And then you get the negative person who says "How do you know you're able to do it? Shure maybe it's in your head?" And shure maybe it is, I dunno. But we do it and it works. Shure a greyhound wouldn't believe in you, you know, or a horse wouldn't believe in you.

We did a stallion two weeks ago. It was a show-jumping stallion and it was lame for three weeks. A man came down from Irishtown called Gerry Slattery. He's one of the top horsemen in Ireland; a real tough man. Like, you wouldn't pull the wool over this lad's eyes 'cos he'd know the ins and outs of a horse. He rang me a week later and said: "I came down in the lorry with a horse to you Gerry and its perfect now, thanks." But then you get people who say like "That's a load of cow shit." And that's their opinion but it's in their minds you see. I don't see why anyone would bother coming to me for help or why I would stand out there using my time if I thought I couldn't help someone. And as for the people I can't help, I'd like to send them on to another person; like there's another healer called Mary Keegan, she does a lot of alternative work, I'd send them to her, or I'd send them to acupuncture. Or a person might have a torn muscle and I'd recommend a physio for them. Sometimes it wouldn't be just your job.

You would often have incidences where you see something in a person that you know you've seen before and you would say "Go back to your GP and they will help you." Ninety-five per cent of them will do their job 100% like, and they're top class people. But for some reason or another, they don't want to recognize Lyme disease. Now, there's a theory for that too but we won't go into it. That's for another day.

Doctors have a plan in place. If they don't know something themselves, they will send you on to a specialist who might send you on to another one and you'll arrive back and know nothing. What I don't understand is that if they've seen something before, shure nine times outa ten they should be able to recognize it. But obviously, it's the State as well a lot of the time. I hear them talking on Joe Duffy about the pain patches. Obviously, people are on them because they're working for them, but now a lot are being taken off them because of the medical card and they're in dire straits. To me, if something was working for somebody and was able to keep them mobile, why would you take it away from them? It doesn't make common sense but then sense is not that common *[laughs]*!

To the likes of the people that charge five-hundred Euro and say they can cure cancer I wouldn't say anything because is there a cure for cancer? I don't know. Can you cure somebody with cancer? I don't believe it. So, a person who would set himself up to say he can do something like that is f***ing crazy. T'wouldn't be for me right! I wouldn't send him a message, I wouldn't even think about him because I hope I'd never be in the situation where I had to go to a person like that. But you take him at five-hundred Euro, then you take all the steroids and the chemo treatments that add up to millions, like millions! So, in a way five hundred mightn't seem an awful lot to try something. The multinational companies they're controlling the world, they are controlling e-v-e-r-y-t-h-i-n-g. To me personally, I wouldn't even comment on it because I don't know.

I don't have a payment system. If a person has a tenner they can give it to me and if they don't, they needn't bother. I never set out to earn money from this. Now, when I do a horse or a dog I have a set payment for them because I give up my day; like I could be above in the shed 'till 12 o'clock at night so you have to get something for it. But we can check a dog for a tenner and do a top-class job and know every bit of its skeleton down, so that's not really charging right?! Not really. Again, because I can't really be… I have no qualifications so I can't say I did this, or I did that. And now the way the world has gone so f***ed up that unless you can write something down with a rake of history behind it, it's not right.

Now a simple thing; if a person was buying or selling a racing dog, they'd often ring me and say "Gerry, what are you at? I'm buying a dog

and I'm paying five thousand for it and I want you to check him." The
first thing I would say is no, and for two reasons. One reason is that
the man that's selling the dog might need that five-thousand Euro to
raise his family. The man that's buying him mightn't want him if there's
an injury that might affect him later and I'm not qualified to make that
decision, so we let the professional people deal with that. I've refused
that thing several times. I wouldn't do it because you cannot step into
somebody else's work. We just do our own simple work and keep it
simple. And we don't want to tell anyone about it. If somebody wants
to use it, they'll use it and we'll do the job to the best of our ability. But
there's certain things you will not do. We know exactly who we are and
we're not going to pretend we're something we are not.

There's a girl coming tonight to me, whose father I've known
for about 25 years, and she told me a story that really put me sharp.
About 25 years ago, this girl's father was selling a dog for ten thousand
which was an awful lot of money for a dog at the time. But the man
who was buying the dog wanted to be sure there was no injuries in him.
So, he brought him to a fellah who would check them over. But when
he'd bend one of his wrists, the dog would start roaring like that. Then
your man said, "There's a bit of a problem here" and wouldn't pass the
dog for the sale. The seller was very disappointed because the sale didn't
go through and the other guy was disappointed because he thought it
was a really good dog. So, there you have a man who wasn't really qualified to do what he was doing but he done it because he chose to put
himself forward. When the man selling the dog returned - and this is
how I got to know him first - there was a neighbour of his and he told
him the story. The neighbour looked at him and said: "Ara Jaysus, go up
to Gort and the butcher will fix that for you in two minutes." So he arrived over and we bent up his wrist and saw the problem straight away;
there was a nerve trapped above on top of his shoulder. And we found
the nerve and released it, went back down to his wrist, bent it up - pain
gone and I said, "Leave him alone now for a week then run him again

next Friday and see how he gets on." The dog went in the following Friday and did a timing of 28:18 and the man ended up getting twenty-thousand Euro for him - double the price. That was massive money that time. So that's why I would never check dogs for sale because I don't have the paperwork behind me. That way you eliminate yourself out of those sort of situations. Even if it was my best friend getting a dog I would say "No, get a professional man to check it."

I love the greyhounds. Yeah, a greyhound is a beautiful animal. And sometimes I see a good trailer coming up here and you know this dog's top class and you might be putting them under a bit of pressure, and it will be doing a bit of roaring and I just say "Jaysus, don't tell me what he cost!" Now the ordinary run-of-the-mill dog, you don't mind adjusting as much but you can't let any of that into your brain; you got to take what's in front of you and do what you have to do. Like we have to pick up a dog's two hind legs and press his pelvis right out and he'll be roaring like shit. If that dog is in the semi-final of the derby and the owner sees that he'll be like "What the f*?k?!" but if that's what you've gotta do, that's what you've gotta do.

There were way more faith healers around once, but they died. There's another butcher in Rathkeale, Joe Williams he does the same work as me. Maurice Lane in Ballylanders he's gone old; he's not working no more. Dan O'Neill, he's maybe over 90. I feel very bad that there's nobody else doing it. There was a man over in Longford; a Costello man, he used to do all the Midlands and he died a few years ago, so I'm crowded out with Midlands people. There's too much work for… if there were guys plotted out around the country it would make the work way easier. But like, I hate doing it during the day when I'm trying to run the shop because the divining is very severe, and you just can't just leave the butchers and come in here and do the other job. It zaps your energy, it zaps all your energy.

A lot of people try to help me with grounding and all that - people who are into reiki, but shure I don't understand it. I never learned nothing about that. Of a Wednesday night I'm just zapped like. So, I go up to Henley's bar and I drink four fast pints and I go to bed *[laughs]* and I work again in the morning; I tear into Thursday. I'd have to of a Wednesday night because you would be seeing so many things during the day that if you didn't switch off your computer brain or dull it that bit it would be going round in your head all night. Like, did I make a mistake, did I look after that person right? You would replay everybody in your head. You need to switch it off.

I'm awful lucky. I have the personality that I don't take anything too seriously. I totally isolate myself from that work. If someone rings me I say, "Yeah we are working tomorrow" and I didn't plan that. It just happened. So, I'm there doing the work but – in my head- it's not me that's doing it. I'm only the gobshite that got the job. You see there'd be more people at it, but they've gone so protective of themselves and they don't want to give their energy to somebody else, they're so all about themselves and so greedy; people are gone terrible like and they don't want to help others. I remember asking one guy to go off and do a blood test. He was riddled with gout and everything and I said, "If you find out your blood type, I'll be able to help you change your diet and get rid of the shit out of your system." So to help him find out his blood type, I said, "The next time you see the van for the auld donating blood, go and donate." And he said, "O Jesus, I wouldn't give that to no one." He was so sucked into himself he wouldn't even donate blood.

I'd say faith healing is dead on the ground, dead on the ground. I can't see the young ones doing it, cos their not grounded; they didn't come from the land, they didn't see hardship - they don't know what hardship is. And are they able to receive or are they able to give? D'you know, I think the computers and everything have their heads fried. I don't know what the future of our job is. Hopefully, there will be other people that will come to my yard someday. There's one girl now who came from America to stay here in Gort; she's studying veterinary and her friend told her about me. She's come three years now to see us working and she'd spend every Monday and Wednesday evening watching us working with the dogs and out doing the horses. She's mad about it and I know that if you got the likes of her, she'd be able to carry it on 'cos she'd give the energy for it and she sees… well, she'd let her mind see what's there. It's just not out of a book with her. She saw more things happen out that backyard with greyhounds and it blew her mind. She'd see the changes that would come over a greyhound in five minutes. It blew her mind and she brought back her brother and her father to see us work. She came first in 2013 when Co. Clare were going well in the hurling and we'd bring her up to watch the matches in Henley's and have a few drinks - a lovely, lovely girl. If you let someone like that, that would have an interest like…

It's all about being able to give your own energy and know that everybody would teach you… every person you treat teaches you for the next person if you let your brain learn. Every day is a school day.

I do a thing on babies called farm a féiste; it's with a rope. It was known one time as a calf knot where people would do it with calves. An old man passed that cure on to me because he saw me doing dogs and he said: "Gerry, you look after this and you give it on to someone who will treat it properly and do it properly." Travelling people use this cure a lot as they could come to any place with a baby who had colic. It's done with three knots and you deliver the positive energy onto the child through the rope which is the medium to transfer it. It's like my divining rod that shows me where the problems are in the person. You make three knots in the rope then hold it over the baby and when you pull it the rope comes clear. It works in horses as well. That's just a cure that is there for generations and generations and there is no science to it, you cannot explain it but unless someone is prepared to carry it on…

Carnoughal is my favourite place. That's where our home house is. I love to go out there every summer. When I was a young fella I used to milk thirty goats every evening before I went butchering and we used to sell the goats in the market in Ennis every Easter Saturday. That was the

Easter Sunday dinner one time; a goat kid. I never drank cows' milk until I went to live in Ennis; we were reared on goats milk every one of us.

When you are living in a place you don't appreciate it at all. It's only when you go away from it…. But I go out to my sister's twice a week and go down to my home house maybe once a month and Jaysus it's just special and the soil there is so rich. You drive in through rocks and then you turn down a boreen and you've the best soil in the world, where you could grow anything. It was a good place to grow up, it was all innocent fun… But unfortunately, now the community in Tubber is… O'Grady's pub was like a rock concert every night when I was growing up and it's now closed. Again because of the bullshit; the drink driving and the no smoking. Pretending that you're doing people and society better - shure they have it destroyed. In the history of the pubs in Tubber nobody ever got killed going home in a car crash. So where are these stats, like? They've all the rules for the good people and no rules for the gougers. One time, when we were children, we used to play cops and robbers and the cops would go after the bad lads. But they leave the bad lads alone now and they target the good people. And we'll leave on that note [laughs].

Human Healing

Tonja Reichley
Herbalist based between Kinvara and Denver

I visited the Burren for the very first time twenty years ago and felt an immediate connection. I was studying to be a herbalist at that time - but there was something that drew me to this specific place; the Burren itself. I came back and began living here eleven years ago. I came in May - we arrived in Bealtaine and so *[laughs]*, I washed my face in the dew - I was totally immersed in the old traditions that I feel like are still alive here. It felt like a coming home - like a place of my roots. I don't know that I had the words then but when I look back on it - I'm probably going to get emotional here - I would recognize people who I'd never met before and I'd be like "Hey, don't I know you?" It just felt like I had found, my roots, my heritage, my lineage. Even though, growing up my parents never talked about Ireland; they weren't Irish; like my ancestors came to America during the famine so it's been a really long time. All I know about my ancestors is that they came from Sligo and the North; Armagh, not from this area - these are the two links we have.

It's mysterious why we're drawn to a place but I knew it in my bones straight away. Like, I was on a Bus Eireann trip from Galway to Doolin that first time going through Kinvara just looking out and thinking "What is this place?" We drove through Ballyvaughan and all the other amazing villages but there was something about Kinvara and this landscape that drew me.

That was before the cliffs became as touristy as they are now.

We rented bikes in Doolin and it was so windy so we were cycling up this hill to get there and it was so crazy *[laughs]* but it was amazing because it was off-season and we went clear out to the edge. I remember going down to one of the shelves and laying there looking 300 feet down and it felt so wild and free.

Now I bring pilgrimage groups here. My philosophy is so much about giving back and when you're on these tourist buses they're just taking pictures and taking so much from the land. When I go to sacred sites or walk on the land anywhere I very much want to offer back but I almost felt like all my energy was being rejected in some places. By giving back I mean just sharing my breath with the land, giving reverence and gratitude and letting the land receive it. You feel a response from the land when you do that except at some of the over-developed tourist sites *[laughs]*. It's startling to me how much some places have closed themselves off energetically. I think these places are just protecting themselves from the taking and the grabbing that masses of tourists just travelling by to take photographs sometimes do.

Corcomroe has been a sacred place for hundreds of years and that energy has been held. There's plenty of coaches, especially in more recent years, that go there yet I think there are enough people who hold a lot of reverence for it and that balances the energy. The first time I went there I heard chanting so that's how strong the energy felt to me; it's still in the memory of that place and we're still able to touch it.

To me, the way to protect places is by not leaving rubbish or cigarette butts, being eco-conscious, eco-aware and treading lightly; staying on the paths. There's been a lot of environmental research about forests and bogs and other places where the eco-systems are being altered or destroyed by the hordes of people going in. In Corcomroe it's important also to not step on the gravestones particularly and I'm glad they've put signs up about this.

I have a dear friend in Galway who is native to Kinvara; he grew up there and he's very in touch with the Irish imagination, culture, history and mythology and he says that, probably, I can get away with saying a lot more things than and Irish person when talking about St Brigid because I'm American. Who knows if it's heard or received or not; that's not why I say it or do it but maybe I can get away with more as I'm not moulded to different viewpoints.

Brigid, to me, is amazing. I refer to her as a bridge and a threshold from pre-Christian tradition to Christian. With what is going on right now with the church in general - the unhealthiness of the church - is that people are again looking at the environment and looking at nature as a way to connect into their spiritual selves. The Christian tradition is still going to be here, it's not going to go anywhere but it's not really healthy right now and there's a lot of questions around it. And so Brigid is helping us just as she did when St Patrick and the other early Christians came to Ireland; she's leading us back to earth and to nature. In her pre-Christian or Goddess component, she's helping us remember these things.

Brigid is the goddess of healing and midwifery and of smithcraft; the fire and forge and poetry and words. I'm particularly drawn to her because of the healing aspect; the midwifery aspect. I look at midwifery also as a pathway to healing. As a herbalist, I don't call myself a healer necessarily because I'm giving people the tools they need to heal themselves; we need to heal ourselves. I look at myself as a midwife to healing. This is different from being a baby midwife; it's about giving them the tools. There's a beautiful word called syncretism; it's about an intermingling of traditions and Ireland has always had that. That's one of the many beautiful things about Ireland is that it has - We do have the Roman Catholic Church but then there are many components of it that are still very pre-Christian and that have echoes of the Celtic and Irish spiritual tradition.

With regards to the transition of Brigid from pre-Christian to Christian I think it was that those Druids who were the Celtic priests and priestesses honouring her knew that this other religion was coming and she was very important to them so she was born in human form. We have record of her birth as an actual human and a record of her death. Brigid means exalted one, or that's one of the definitions that I know of. And then there's other Brigids that kind of just kept more that title aspect. Some of the old myths from pre-Christian Brigid transferred over to Christian Brigid like the fire temple in Kildare which is a beautiful example. This fire looked over by the druid priestesses and later the nuns stayed lit until the times of Cromwell. I think it was a magical flame and I believe that even when Brigid was in human form in the 5th Century no fuel was added to the fire and no ash was produced so that magic continued from pre-Christian use. And Brigid, of course, had her favourite herbs; dandelion, blackberry, ladies mantle.

After visiting Ireland for a while, I found a teacher who lives in Mullingar now who's American too but is pretty well-known in Ireland; she's been here for 20 years. Like me, she has ancestry here although her ancestry is more immediate. I studied with her and then started comparing the herbs that grow where I am in America and the herbs that grow here. Herbalists have what is called a materia medica; that's our medicine bag of herbs that we go to for anything from cancer to the common cold to menstrual issues, fertility or whatever. My core materia medica is twenty-five herbs and all of these are here in this land that my DNA is from. I don't know if it's big here but in America, you can get

St. Brigid's Statue, Liscannor

your DNA analysed and they can tell you your ancestry. It's very telling that a lot of us in America are really wanting to know our roots. I mean we've been there for 300 years and very few genealogies go back more than that which is nothing in the whole scope of our human body and what we know. And so, back to my materia medica, the herbs that I work with are herbs that grow here and also grow in Denver, where I'm from and many of them are herbs that we bought when we - my ancestors came over. The Europeans brought things like dandelion, meadowsweet, plantain, and mullein to America. These are all things that people might refer to as weeds yet some of them are our most powerful medicines.

Folk herbalists, which is what I refer to myself as, believe that our healers are right outside our back door. Not that turmeric isn't amazing; turmeric is an eastern spice, and maybe it would have made its way here but it doesn't grow here.

Our bodies are aching and yearning for nourishment; spiritual nourishment, physical nourishment and these herbs will give all of us that. They're filled with trace vitamins and minerals so that they'll nourish us deeply. Not that these other herbs such a turmeric won't help relieve symptoms; they're powerful - they're just not our native European or native Irish tradition. And from local produce you don't just get deep nourishment but there's also the weaving together of community elements. Since the Celtic Tiger we have become more isolated from community so just going back to buying from our local farmer and being able to make tea from nettles that are growing in your back garden - there's nothing like it.

Folk healers believe that what our ancestors have used for thousands of years is what our bodies are craving. We don't break down the herbs into isolated constituents; we can recognise those constituents and we know how they work on a specific body. I work primarily with teas as this is what I feel our bodies are aching for; they recognise teas. That's how our ancestors have been taking herbs for thousands of years. Tinctures are newer; I will work with tinctures some but I do not work with capsules or tablets. Some folk herbalists might do if that's what you need to start to get compliance because it's what a lot of people want; something that is just quick and easy. Making a cup of herb tea is kind of like buying from the local farmer and the nourishment you get from just doing that - engaging with yourself and taking 5 or 10 minutes versus just swallowing a tablet or supplement - is wonderful.

But, with regards to the DNA I have some black Americans who are my students so when we learn about folk herbalism it's not meant to be exclusive by any means and I'm sure there would be a Chinese folk herbalist who would be happy to treat me - I'm just talking about using our own ancient very traditional remedies to heal.

I learned about the Irish traditions through a lot of self-study. I have been very intrigued with Ireland before I even visited here and my teacher in Mullingar would have also introduced it to me. Also, when I studied herbs in the States you'd hear about Bealtaine and other traditions and they resonated with me very deeply. So I've looked at how what we call the wheel of the year not only encompasses the year but the life, the day and the breath. Each breath we take aligns us like that springtime, that newness when we're inhaling and that stillness between the breaths if we focus. The four-part breath you do in yoga is the wheel or the cycle so it's really beautiful and connecting in that way.

I've also read a lot of mythology like Lady Gregory and Lady Wilde and the Celtic twilight and William Butler Yeats, so I've read a lot of the early books on folklore, spells, remedies and cures. But I think we're at a whole other layer of losing. This always happens with every generation that dies but now we're losing the living memory of these ancient cures and folk methods of healing. I think people can now see there are different options available apart from what I call the allopathic route - people call it traditional medicine but it's not - *[laughs]*. They see what I'm doing and what the other Burren healers are doing and so a lot of people are shifting. Healing is in the land, healing is in the water, good food and in the earth. I feel really positive about this but moderation in all things; we don't need to get really over the top with it all.

I know there can be this tendency for people when they start looking at alternative remedies to just transfer that need that the allopathic or the medical system provided so then they're putting all that weight on Reiki or reflexology. I think people need to be empowered to take health into their own hands and find it all around them - looking within themselves and going back to the land for that healing versus just going to another healer.

I think if the change is going to be sustainable it has to be

Hazelnuts

grassroots; just by creating a community and being in the community. It's not going to be this mass shift because that would be artificial and unsustainable. It will come through creating awareness, writing books and empowering people to participate again. We don't as a culture participate; we don't participate in our healthcare but instead go to a doctor or herbalist and say "What do I take? OK, I'll take it." And we're not participating in our communities or the environment. Especially as women; I don't want this to be a gender thing yet I think we, as women, have always tended to the earth. Sharon Blackie, an English psychologist wrote a book called "If Women Rose Rooted" and it resonates very deeply with me because she wrote on this theme of returning to our connection with the earth; being on the earth, walking on the earth, tending to the earth. She writes about this as being the way that we can participate again and shift back from consumer mentality which is what we're doing when we're taking the tablet from the doctor or the herbalist or the reflexologist. Like "I need my appointment every week to have reflexology but then I'm going to go home and eat a burger and consume a lot of plastic and drive when I could have walked.

So, it's not just about one thing, I think. And it can be baby steps; we can sometimes feel overwhelmed like "How is it ever going to change?" But by living very authentically from your place, engaging with the earth, with the rhythms and the seasons, with what's growing right outside your back door you can do that.

When people first taste nettle that's freshly harvested it's so delicious if we would only give it a chance. It's a process just even getting to that place that *[laughs]* when someone comes by you say "OK, can I serve you a cup of nettle tea that I've harvested whilst walking the dog?" Most people would run a mile! It's not going to happen overnight; it's about baby steps and fostering that sense of participation. It's a tricky one, it is.

With regards to the future, I feel like we're in a really positive place. I feel people are starting to look back again. I don't mean to be totally pessimistic - this is an amazing time to be alive as well - but we are seeing now what isn't working and looking back to see what did. And there's a longing for things that our mothers or grandmothers did that we would once have been like "No! I want to get to the city and I want to have a car and a big fancy home." But now we are going back to the simple things.

It won't happen overnight but I do feel that the education of people is what's going to slowly shift it. Just by helping people be aware that there are still these living traditions that are really precious and finding the courage to create conversation and gatherings around this. And we need to plant the seed. Maybe this is easier for me, being an American; I can be really open here because I've not been pigeon holed. But you can have a discussion about these kinds of things with someone who is skeptical. It might take them 5 more years to go see a bonesetter; maybe doing Reiki is the easiest one for them at this point.

One day I will be that old woman in a cottage in the Burren making potions or tea or essential oils *[laughs]* and until then I'll be gathering that information and keeping it alive and keeping the memory of these treasures.

My daughter is thirteen and she loves taking to people whenever she comes here; she's a writer. Once she did this thing called 'The People of Kinvara'. It's based on the huge social media thing called 'The People of New York'. Basically what my daughter did is to record a 5 or 10-minute interview with older people in Kinvara, draw a story out of them and post it on Facebook. In the schools - I feel like community engagement between elders and children is happening again though it could happen more. And young people are maybe more open to the idea of herbal remedies.

I think that with health we often look for one type of cure to replace the other instead of finding a pathway that leads us by the holy wells and past the fairy trees and across the landscape of the Burren rather than from one clinic to another.

I do herbal pilgrimages around the Burren where we focus on the herbs and go to the sacred sites. We start each morning with a circle and have a theme for the day. Our first stop is St Coleman's holy well at Eagle's Rock and there we engage with the land and learn about the plants. On the way to the holy well, there's normally guardians and there's that hawthorn tree that's right before the entrance and so I'm teaching them about connecting to the trees and the landscape as we're giving reverence to these places and receiving the healing in return.

The groups we take are very small, which is really important to me; like 6 is my largest. But even with 6, it's a production to do things like get in and out of the van which can take fifteen minutes. I really like to go to these out-of-the-way places but I'm aware of the literal as well as figurative footsteps that we're leaving.

The people who come on the pilgrimages are herbalists but also people that just love Ireland and want to experience it in a really intimate way. Mainly they are Americans but I have had some Canadians, Australians, and French.

I have been leading these pilgrimages for ten years and so I've done a lot of personal growing and reflecting. When I began I thought it to be more about what happens at places like St Brigid's well in Liscannor; like you do this thing in reverence and it may or may not be painful - you have to struggle as it's a spiritual journey of some sort. But I now feel pilgrimage is about helping us remember how to participate again. When people come on pilgrimage with me we live in a community for seven days. That's unique and it's not easy in this day and age to share and to be with a group of people that you don't know or have just met. We're out in these high-energy places all day and it's about gratitude and giving and then we normally have dinner together. So pilgrimage, to me, is about participation; not taking but giving and when you're giving you receive so much more. It's also about releasing expectations so you allow yourself to be totally present with reverence and gratitude. It can be a journey that's about learning a way of living life as well.

P.J. Curtis
Music Producer and Son of Horse Healer from Kilnaboy

I was born at the end of the war and for the first 10 years of my life here I lived in the old world. We had no transport, there was nothing mechanical and farming was done by the old ways. Hay was saved by hand, turf was cut by hand and drawn home by horses. Transport was the horse and because my father was a smith and a healer of horses there were always a lot around. From the '40s my mother ran a little country store. She was also a musician and my father was a bit of a storyteller so we were continuously surrounded by people in this place here. It was a cúirting or a rambling house as well; outside business hours people would come; the men would play cards and when my mother's people came there was music. She had aunts and uncles who were musicians; they were Lynches. They would all play so when they arrived the fiddle would come out And that was my first introduction to music; under the table here aged two or three, listening to my mother play fiddle with her mother and uncle. I can still hear the tunes. It was such a powerful time that stood me forever with a hunger for music.

The school was literally up the yard so that first ten years was all the old ways; everything was done as it had been for hundreds of years until the '50s when electricity came in. When electricity came I suppose it could be said that everything changed. It made life a damn-side easier for my mother when she could switch on a light rather than have to work the gas lamp and you could press another switch and a fire could come on -an electric fire and the cooker was an amazing thing to her so life became easier.

We had a battery radio, what I now call a 'black and white radio' *[laughs]*. So, you had a wet battery and a dry battery; one of them ran out pretty quick I can tell you. The wet battery would have to be taken into Corofin to be recharged and that meant several days of no radio - I had a fear of that because I had become very quickly addicted to radio. I remember my mother had taught me to read but with the radio, it was like music coming in from outer space. It was from the American Forces Network (AFN) in Germany. The AFN broadcast from Stuttgart to the American troops still in Germany post-war. They were broadcasting to Southern army guys and playing blues and jazz and the first programme that turned me on is the grand old opera of Nashville Tennessee. I was relating to the music in a way I didn't fully understand but now I see I was relating to music that was here in the house at home because country music is Irish music that went to the Appalachians hundreds of years ago. And now here I was listening to the music of our forebears. So, then I was hearing blues and I was only ten - and how does someone of ten get so obsessed by this music?

My outer life was running around barefoot in the summer. I think I must've known every cave, hole and recess in the Burren - in fact I was trapped and one for a long time until someone came and released me but that's another story.

When I was growing up you saw calves being born, you saw cattle die, you saw people die. When our neighbour next door was on his last legs I was taken into the house to watch the death. Because it was understood that this was real life and you were being trained in it right away. There was nothing cynical about it or clinical about it; it was preparing a young fella for real life. Like the killing of a pig - which I hated, I absolutely hated and I would run - I was still running from it at twelve or thirteen. At this stage, they didn't have humane killers where the pig was shot and fell over. This was when the pig's throat was cut, or they drove a spike through his forehead - once it hit his brain he was dead but there was a lot of suffering. There was one man that would come to kill a pig and he'd strike a blow, then he'd take a puff of his pipe and continue telling a story - he was very cruel. There was a sense of cruelty about it - it was as if the animal didn't deserve a clean death nor did they have any feelings. Then he'd strike another blow, and the pig would be screaming with the spike going in through his forehead. Sometimes he'd miss and the spike would hit his skull and it could be minutes before the act was carried out and the pig would die. At least the cutting of the throat would be quick but I hated all that, so I would do a disappearing act when the pig was being killed.

My father had a lot of herbal knowledge - he made all of his own potions, one that is in a story in my book, had thirteen ingredients that he would rattle off, he didn't have it written down. And the names were in old Latin which meant that probably these cures came from the monks in the 12th-century abbeys - the healers would have been within those communities and how it got out to us I don't know. But then we had always known that the smith had some healing gifts.
I never felt that magic out with my father when he was doing the healing. But I was interested - he used to take me out with him from the time I was about 8 years of age. I probably enjoyed it more for the travel because we had no car and a car would come to collect him and we could be as far away as Milltown Malbay or Kilrush or maybe even as

far as South Galway. I remember once we went up to Ballyvaughan and the car we were in took fire and we couldn't get out of it *[laughs]*. And I remember the driver saying, "Get under the seat!" as if that was going to save me if the car exploded *[laughs]*. But I loved going out on the trips with my father because it was a day out. When my father was doing the horsey thing - curing the horse - the farmer's wife would often bring me in and give me a cup of tea and apple tart or sixpence because my father would take no money.

But then when I got a bit older I was there to help him. I remember when I was eleven one of the things I would have to do is hold the jar to collect the blood - it was a jam jar. My father would bleed the horses from the jugular. He would cut the jugular not all the way through but just a little with the lance and a hammer and the blood would come spurting out. He would leave the blood sitting there and whatever way it would separate he would be able to figure out what was wrong and administer a cure accordingly. He had learned that from his father. I would catch the blood, leave the jar to the side and then hand him a pin- a normal safety pin - he would take a piece of the horses hair and lay it on the wound because the blood was still coming at this stage and he would fold the horses skin over the wound and pin it with the safety pin which had been dipped in alcohol to sterilise it. And so, the horse's hair was lying directly on the wound and it would be bonding it. Sometimes, if he was in a barn, he would use spiderweb to bond the cut.

Once, when I was holding my little jar the horse pulled back or whatever and the blood spurted onto my face and into my eyes and my mouth and so I swallowed the blood and my whole front was covered in it because this was serious spouting from the jugular - I was eight or nine at the time. The farmer's wife came and wiped me clean but that night I had a terrible dream about being steeped in blood and I woke up covered in sweat. After that day I don't think I ever wanted to go out with my father again - it was so traumatic. Since that, I've had a terrible fear of blood. It's only in the last couple of years with all this business of being ill with my heart that I'm able to not pass out when I have a blood sample taken; I have that much horror of it.

From that moment on I would see to it I was gone when he wanted me to go with him. But I think my father had been trying to train me for the healing; he was always saying "Watch this, look out for that, don't worry about the horse." He was already preparing me to accept what he had to give. A lot of it was not written down and that's why he hated to see me reading books that he thought were softening the brain. Everything that he learned about farming, about the horse healing, about the forge was passed on orally. But I didn't learn it and so the cure didn't ever pass down.

There was really a break there with my father when he began to see that I was showing no interest in farming, in the forge and in being with him out on his healing trips. I was more interested in my books, listening to music and learning to play the guitar than anything here. I couldn't wait to get out of the place. When I was sixteen I went off playing with bands.

I hated Ireland and thought I'd never come back. My brothers were different; they were natural farmers. I often thought why didn't he give them the cure? Maybe he didn't see it in them. But I felt that he knew the day of the horse on the landscape was over. People didn't need horses anymore; they weren't ploughing, they weren't cutting hay, they weren't travelling. In the '50s there would be a queue outside here of traps down into our yard when people would tie them up and walk to the church because that's how people travelled - by trap or by sidecar; nobody had motorcars. There were only two people who had cars in the locality and that was the teacher and the priest.

But this was to do with time as well. My two brothers became farmers but things were changing - in the late '50s and early '60s more farms became motorised; they had tractors, they had cars, the need for horses wasn't as acute. And only people who had horses just because they loved them would come to my father. But he was still going out curing them 'til the day he died.

I believe I have a power but then we all have the power to tune into energy. When I left primary school, I had to cycle over twelve miles every day into the Christian Brothers in Ennis where I'd get the crap beaten out of me by those sadists who shouldn't have been let anywhere near kids. After I got home and the work about the place was done I could go to my hideouts in the caves and trees where I kept my books. That's how I got in tune with being alone and attuned to the music of the Burren. If you listen you'll realise the Burren is never silent. Since I've come back, in my older years, to live here I've rekindled some of that - of being open to all the energies of the birds and animals. But we become adults and I can't help that some of me is now cynical - it's a hardening of the soul - but I don't want to be like that. We have to let the light in. Have you ever thought of sound as colour? I hear sound in colour. In the recording studio, working as a producer, I experience each sound as having a different shading from deep dark to light - It's like I'm mixing my herbs.

How do you explain something that can't be touched or felt but yet you walk through it every day? I live in the home of my ancestors. People say there is a good energy here. It was built in the 1700s and has had its fair share of tragedy with 5 of my father's family dying in their beds in 1919. When I first returned I could sense an energy in Mullaghmór that I couldn't explain but I just knew I wanted to save it. I thought that if I tried to describe what I felt I would have sounded like a loony. But another guy I met living around here said he felt the same - he thought maybe he was going mad until he started to find other people of the same mind. We set up the Burren Action Group to stop the interpretative centre being built by Mullaghmór because we somehow understood that the constant trail of huge coaches would upset the natural flow. It's not that we don't want visitors there, of course, it's a beautiful place and people should see it but we just wanted people to come to the nearby town of Corofin and then maybe take a small bus to the mountain. Simply getting off a coach, taking a picture and then getting back on devalues a place somehow; that's not experiencing the Burren - gentle tourism should be the way. As soon as you put a camera to your eye you're not in the present - you have divorced yourself from that moment. It is the same for me working with music; the instant you put a microphone in front of someone you're breaking the magic between the music and you. We filter and transmit energy as does the radio; we are the magic box through which energy is received.

Nowadays we are, so many of us, looking for a guru. We're looking for a magic formula to be handed to us. But I believe that there's no nirvana in this world. It's all about being content with your lot. My parents had that. When you accept your lot and say, "This is where I'm at; today was a good day and tomorrow will take care of itself." then all will be well.

Curtis Family Radio

Pádraic Ó Máille
Trainer, Facilitator & Healer from New Quay via Galway

I'm from Galway city and the first time I ever came across mention of faith healing is when I would visit my cousins in Carrantrila in North Galway. At Stations and wakes and weddings I'd hear the older people whisper that 'that lad has the gift.'

My father had died before I was born and there was a belief that when this happened the child would have the ability to cure thrush. Right from the very get go it was something I resisted like the plague. At six, seven and eight years of age the last thing a kid wants is to be in any way different to your peers.

My cousin, May Coen, however was a wise and erudite lady and did reassure me that indeed I had a cure but there was no reason for me to use it.

The first time I actually applied it was when I was eleven. An aunt of mine, herself from a revered medical family, beseeched me to say a prayer over her year-old son who had thrush for ages and had kept them from sleeping. It had resolutely resisted the most potent antibiotics of the time. My immediate response was that this was stupid and I wasn't doing it but because of my deepest respect for my aunt I relented. Despite my misgivings, utter reluctance and complete disbelief in the process I muttered a prayer over the cousin, blew on his face and lo and behold the thrush vanished within hours.

For years after I kept my cure to myself, and living in the city, there was no call or knowledge for my services. Many years later at a family confirmation in my in-laws, my father-in-law, sheepishly took me aside and asked me if I wouldn't mind blowing on his throat as he was in agony with thrush.

Now here was one of the most intelligent and wise men that I'd ever met. As a former Adjutant-General in the Irish Army he was one of the first Officers to successfully bring a battalion to Congo and have them all return safely. I can recall saying to him 'Pat, you're not serious, you don't believe in that mullarkey of piseiog and superstition!'

He assured me that undoubtedly I had a cure and that he'd be more than grateful if I tried it. His son, also a consultant doctor, had him on antibiotics all week and to no avail. I'd had a few drinks, muttered a prayer, blew in his mouth and returned to the party. Later that evening he gratefully informed me that the thrush had cleared without trace.

I was always a tad ambivalent as to the efficacy of the cure on the basis that those I did cure, or at least those close to them, believed implicitly in the cure. There was always the whiff of the power of the placebo.

I guess what really confirmed the power of the healing for me was a case where the lady wasn't conscious when I visited her. She was a beautiful neighbor of ours in Clare and as she was nearing her final journey she developed a severe bout of thrush. Her family asked me to visit her and when I called to Cahercalla hospital she just so happened to be on her own whilst her family went out for tea. She was peaceful, but totally unconscious and at least overtly, unaware and oblivious of my presence. I stayed with her awhile and gently blew on her thrush. Before I was back in New Quay her family had called to know if I'd been there because the thrush had completely vanished. This for me was proof positive that some dynamic, presumably of supernatural origins was playing out in this.

Some years ago I was summoned by a lady called Mrs. McHugh from McHugh's pub in Carnmore in County Galway to meet her. She was a great age but utterly lucid and fascinating. Like me, her father had died before her birth, and she practiced the cure all her life.

I was intrigued to meet her because I'd never met anyone with the cure myself and as such, had no induction or initiation into the ritual of healing. She was totally convinced of the potency of the cure and was very adamant that I practice my cure profusely. She had served a lifetime as proprietor of her public house and had cured hundreds of people throughout the years. Her method was similar to mine in that it involved blowing on the person and reciting a prayer. She reminded me most clearly that there was to be no payment extorted for the healing. She was in no doubt that those with a cure be obliged to use it and that the world needed this. It's said that the proof of the pudding is in the eating and when my own dog Potter became lame for a number of weeks I first took him to a Vet and after a rigorous examination I was not overly impressed with the diagnosis that the dog lose some weight. Needless to say the dog didn't improve from this intervention and in some degree of desperation I took him to the bone setter, Gerry O'Donoghue in Gort. Now there's an alchemist of a higher order.

Without as much as looking at the dog or examining him he proclaimed that the dog had fractured his third metacarpal; that there was no immediate cure for it; but it wasn't serious and it would heal in time. In fascination I asked him how he knew and he said. 'Feel it for yourself, there's a growth over the third metacarpal on his front right paw.' And sure enough there was. And with time it healed perfectly.

I recall later googling a scientific article on the 'Long-term Prognosis of Metacarpal and Metatarsal Fractures in Dogs' and after 2200 words of academic rhetoric the learned scientists concluded that 'according to the present study, these empirical and often repeated recommendations (scientific ones) cannot be confirmed or refuted statistically.' What a load of seafóid (nonsense) and unnecessary suffering to perpetrate on our beloved canine community. Mrs. McHugh was indeed right. There is a very real place for healing even in the midst of unparalleled scientific breakthroughs. Gerry explained to me afterwards that thrush was one of the more receptive ailments to cures and that a faith healer in Gort had successfully worked with local GPs there for years in treating the condition. I'm often asked what my real views on healing are. My response is that everything has an energy. In Conamara it's said that 'aithníonn ciaróg ciaróg eile' or in the English equivalent 'birds of a feather flock together' and even in the less eloquent scientific version it's acknowledged that 'like attracts like.' So it is with energy. Like energy attracts like energy. And everything indisputably has an energy.

Health has an energy. So too sickness and disease. Poverty has an energy. So also has abundance, riches and wealth. Most powerfully, the people you're surrounded by exude an energy. The great American writer Jim Rohn said that 'you're the average of the five people you're surrounded by the most.' This wisdom has the capacity to change your life if heeded.

Rohn suggests three strategies. Firstly sever your association with toxic people. There's no doubt misery loves company and there's a thriving community trading in it. Every quarterly successive JNLR report testifies to the enduring popularity of Joe Duffy's 'Liveline' programme. It's the only radio programme that consistently increases its listenership. This is proof positive of our national penchant for bitching and moaning and griping.

Secondly, limit your association with people who may have a negative impact on aspects of your energy levels. I recall once my late Mother asking me what I was doing that day and when I told her I was giving a talk in front of twenty-five business people she had immediate apoplexy which perpetrated an instant state of terror in me. 'What happens if you forget your lines? What happens if you run out of things to say? What happens if they ask you a question you don't know?'

The reality was that my Mother had never spoken in front of a large crowd and was petrified at the very thought of it. In her association with her terror, and in her worry and concern for me, she unwittingly succeeded very effectively in transferring that fear to me. Having just succeeded in managing the ordeal I made a deal with my Mother that evening. 'Ma, I will never, ever, ever ring you again before an important meeting but I promise you, I'll ring you the second it's over.' It worked swimmingly for thirty years. Remember, sometimes those that love you the most can be unknowingly influencing your energy for the worse.

Finally, Rohn exhorts that we expand our association with positive people. Get around people who uplift your mind, set your heart racing and turn you on.

In addition to people stories and words also radiate a massive energy. Words like tranquility and peace and serenity instantly convey and induce that sense. You can instantly alter your state of mind by changing your habitual words and stories.

A wonderful Irish word with radiant

Burren Limestone at Blackhead

energy is the word 'smacht.' Literally translated it means discipline or control or even mastery. I genuinely believe that discipline is the bridge between aspiration and accomplishment. Every significant achievement in your life was proceeded by discipline or smacht. As a baby you crawled before you walked. You gurgled before you talked and took dozens of times to learn to tie your shoes. But it never occurred to you as a baby to give up. You had inbuilt smacht hardwired into your very DNA.

As we get older however the inherent allure of smacht is replaced by a mentality of the quick fox, the band-aid solution and desert before dinner. It's the 'borrow now pay later' ideology so much beloved of the consumer society. Unfortunately it violates natural principles and ultimately ends up wreaking more trouble than it seeks to avoid.

The statistics don't lie. Two thirds of the Irish population are now overweight with a third obese. 40% of first-time marriages now flounder. And 65% of those retiring will have insufficient funds to tide them in their increasing life expectancy. As John Gray once said 'In our bodies we are accumulating disease. In our relationships toxicity. And in our businesses debt.'

Each of these statistics have at their core one quality; smacht. Failure is not one cataclysmic event that happens overnight. Neither is success for that matter. Each are the result of a cumulative series of disciplines or lack of disciplines practiced over an extended period of time.

I'll finish with the words with the late, great Jim Rohn. "We must all suffer from one of two pains: the pain of discipline or the pain of regret. The difference is discipline weighs ounces while regret weighs tons."

All you need is smacht.

Holy Well at Coscéim

CHAPTER 2
WELLS WHICH MAKE US WELL

The Land, the Water and the Remedies

W hat about the preciousness of wells? In his 1910 publication on the folklore of Clare, T.J. Westropp writes;

"With the usual wise tactfulness of the ancient Irish missionaries all that was harmless was adopted into the new religion, and the wells lost none of their old observances and honour."

Westropp lists a number of wells in the Burren and their cures among which are those used for sore eyes such as Gleninagh which has a 15th Century well-house and the well of Inghean Baoith at

Kilnaboy. He also mentions Colmáin's well between Corcomroe and the Uchtmáma churches which, he says, cure sufferers of 'the pearl' with the films falling off the eyes at the third washing. I can only muse that the pearl refers to what we now know as cataracts. As with today offerings were made to wells in the form of rags, necklaces, buttons or figurines. Pilgrims tied these rags, representing their ailments, to a tree near to or overhanging the well in the belief that the tree would then spirit away their ills.

These wells were considered sacred and Westropp recounts tales where water stolen from them would not boil. One story tells of how when the well at Uchtmáma was offended it closed and broke out lower down the hillside.

Despite attempts by the church hierarchy to implement church baptisms, holy wells were used for this purpose throughout middle ages. In 'The Cambridge History of Ireland', Colmán Ó Clabaigh cites a story about a woman who is cured from breast cancer after receiving a kiss from someone who has been newly baptised. It's been speculated that there was little magic in these things and people living without clean water in smoke-filled botháns surely felt some sort of cure from washing their eyes in pure water that sprang from underground. But it's interesting to speculate that the well which lies equidistant on the short journey between Uchtmáma's three churches and Corcomroe may not have been needed for drinking water in that both settlements had functional drinking wells.

Most famous in the Burren are the three wells that run through the town of Lisdoonvarna. As early as the 1700's, Lisdoonvarna's natural sulphur well was attracting visitors. Cyril Ó Céirín in his introduction to 'A Handbook To Lisdoonvarna and its Vicinity' tells us that its success was so continuous that a hotel and sub post office were built there so the privileged class could reap the benefits at a time when the masses were starving their way through the great famine. The Spa town with its grand hotels grew around its three wells, one of which was found to contain sulphur and with the grant from the local landlord, a kinsman of Westropp, the people came together to build a pump house and bath house for the commercial venture. Ó Céirín mentions a local man whose grandfather was evicted at the time saying 'sourly' the visitors all badly needed the cleansing effects of the sulphur after long winters spent eating too much salt beef and drinking too much bad whiskey.' The wells arose much scientific interest and, like many spa towns, boomed in the 19th Century due to the Victorian enthuasism for building railways. Later, a doctor was brought in to live in the grounds of the bath house and issue prescriptions containing advised quantities of sulphur and magnesium to bathe in or imbibe as well as recommen-dations of walks to take in the fresh, clean Burren air. The spa tradition across Europe brought its own developments as romances blossomed between the visiting family members. Every September, Lisdoonvarna now celebrates the world-famous matchmaking festival which, for good or bad, is a huge draw card for visitors. Whilst long stays at the spa wells died off during the rise of the sun holiday in the 1970's, a local committee is working on a revival of this place where science and natu-ral medicine come together.

Mena Griffin
Faith holder from Lisdoonvarana

Padre Pio's my man. My mother had great devotion to him. She used to write to him for years and send out linen and he'd bless it and send it back to her. And when she'd get it back she'd cut it up and give it to all the people that would be sick. And some of them were cured with it. My husband and I got married in '63 but we had no family until '73. So, of course, we were praying to Padre Pio and my mother was praying for us. Then I had a little girl and after that I had triplets. We were living here at the time but the doctor sent me to Dublin for the birth. Professor De Valera, Eamon De Valera's son was my doctor up there. They thought it was twins we were having but they got the two boys out and the next thing the girl came. So there was three. And it was marvellous. We were kept for six weeks above in Dublin and then we got the brainwave to bring them down to Shannon by plane. It was real warm weather that time in 1976 so you couldn't have taken them in a car. And then I had another girl. It's 42 years now since they were born like. They're all married except we have one boy at home. And to this day we pray. If there's anything wrong people would ring me and say, "Light a candle Mena and say a prayer." They would know I had great devotion to Padre Pio. So I do that. And I have a list down in the kitchen of anyone who asked me to pray for them and I have a picture of Padre Pio and I light a candle every morning for them. We have been to St Giovanni where Padre Pio is from. I've been over three times and my husband Peter has been twice. The kids got us a present for our 50th wedding anniversary of a trip out there and that was great. Shure, it's absolutely brilliant and lovely to get to see his body and all that d'you know. His body used to be in a kind of crypt but they took it up and he was still there to the good and they have him now in front of an altar. In the book I got the other day, he's in front of an altar and you can see him. He looks perfect; just the same as the day he died.

The young people these days - I don't think they want to go to mass or do anything. But if something's wrong, I'm telling you, they won't be long asking you to pray for them or give them something. Maybe in years to come they will go back to the church hopefully.

I go to the well in Liscannor on St Brigid's day every year to get the holy water and give a bottle to different farmers who are relations for their cattle and sheep and all that. They would just go into the slatted house and shake the holy water on the cows and the calves and also on the land. You can't beat the holy water. Every time they go out the door here, I say, "Take the holy water" and they do.

The priest says mass in the church every St Brigid's day, and 'tis

Holy Well, Liscannor

absolutely beautiful. He gives a lovely little sermon and in the middle of mass he brings out a lamb under his arm because it's the first day of spring and he talks about him and that. A real live lamb who's only a few days old. And the church is packed. He leaves out a cloth on the bushes the night before St Brigid's day and the dew comes on that - that's for St Brigid's day then. And he has a man on each door going out and he just leaves it on top of your head, d'you know, to bless you like. And then you have to go through this kind of ring and it's supposed to bring you great luck to go through it. It's made of rushes. And the week before they send out lots of rushes to the neighbours who make the crosses and sell them. Last year they sent out seven cows to Haiti or someplace out foreign with the money they collected from the crosses - three Euros a cross. It would cost a thousand at least for a cow. So they'd make all that money with the crosses, it's really marvellous.

I suppose a lot of people still have got the medals in their cars, especially the old people. But the young people, I don't know that they believe in anything and it's a pity. Even my grandchildren when I put the holy water on them as they're going out the door; I don't know at all if they understand what it is or if they're taught at school or what. You'd be hoping they'd say their prayers but they'd only laugh at you. But I would still do it. The nuns used to leave miraculous medals into the church here. And I've another friend that's very good. She's over 80 now but she used to play the organ in the church and still has great devotion. She'd leave miraculous medals or beads in a box in the church and if you wanted one you could help yourself. It was a good idea especially when there's new babies as you'd give them the miraculous medals. It was more St Christopher before but Padre Pio took over. Anyone that has a new car now, I give them the stickers: Try to keep up the little bit of devotion. And then we have a prayer group every first Wednesday night of the month where we say the rosary and the Padre Pio prayer and then you can say whatever prayers you want yourself. We used to have ten or twelve or more maybe coming to it and now it's down to 4 or 5. You see, we had a lovely lady that died suddenly - she was a great woman for the church so she's gone now. And my friend Chris was sick for the past month with the flu so she wasn't there. There's only a few that come now but we try to keep it going.

Padre Pio would wear the mitten because he had the stigmata in his two hands and his side. And I suppose he had a good lot of them because he'd have to be changing them very often. And the priest there gave them to different people. 'Tis all covered in, you can't take it out of the cellophane thing but 'tis lovely to have that. And then, when my husband used to bring me over to Galway; there's a lady there that has the Padre Pio mitten and she'd give it to me for a few nights if I wanted. I'd always try and have something here in the church for that so we used to get a priest and he'd say mass or the rosary and then he'd bless everybody with the mitten. That was lovely. When they were being blessed with the mitten some people would feel really warm when it was left on your head or you might get whatever you were asking for. Sometimes the perfume would be all around and that was a sign your prayers were answered.

Fr Michael Fitzgerald from Cork came up a few times to us and blessed everybody with the mitten. And t'was lovely. He would have exposition and then say the mass. But you see, it's so hard to go to Galway now and my husband wouldn't drive that much anymore. So we'll just have to try and keep going without it. When I got married we used to have a B&B in the town. In those days, the sulphur wells were open and people used to come from around the country to take the waters. I used to go there myself and a woman would massage your legs and it was great.

Now we have the people coming for the matchmaking festival. In the early days that was just a thing for the tourists but now there's music and dancing everywhere. And we have the refugees from Syria living in that place that used to be a hotel. They are nice. Some of them wave when they walk past on the street and we wave back to them.

Matchmaker Museum

I believe the thing with the wells will go on forever. Every year without fail they come to St Brigid's well and do the rounds. So 'tis lovely. They used to have mass there but I think for health and safety reasons now he has the mass in the church and shure it's always cold and windy that day. I just love to go there every year. Like, if we were passing down, I'd run in and say a few prayers inside. 'Tis lovely to do. Some people are hardly able to walk and they go in there and get down on their knees to get their holy water.

My husband's from Doolin and his mother and father lived in a small little house. When the Aran Island crowd used to come in they'd stay with them if it was a bad night and they couldn't go back. And that would be always to go to St Brigid's well on February 1st. But then you see people are old now and some are dead and gone. You'd wonder how long we'll be able to keep doing it. But we will as long as we're able, please God. My children wouldn't use the wells. I suppose they might run into them to see them but that's all. As for praying; they wouldn't. But if there was a family with a sick person, they'd go every year. And that's why I go every year; because I promised I would. Because An-nette, one of the triplets used get that sickness; like she'd go to sleep - a kind of epilepsy. But she got better and I said, "I will go to the well every year." I didn't leave a picture of her there because you see, there'd be so many that would know her and she wouldn't like that. But thank God all's well now and she has three children of her own. But I still keep going. And I'd often say to her "I'm going because of you." But, I don't know... it doesn't sink in. I have a sister who is very religious too but she's not as much a Padre Pio fan as I am you know. she's always praying, always lighting candles. Shure 'tis a good thing I suppose… I think so.

Lisdoonvarna

Shane Connolly
Farmer and Walking Guide
from Ballyvaughan

I've been running my family's suckling and sheep farm since 1993. Years ago, I found a record of our family farm in Ballyvaughan dating back to the 1820's but I don't know how far back we went before that. I got the info from a record of the tithes - the money you had to pay to the Protestant church. Good Protestants that we were *[laughs]*! My grandmother's side were Murphys from the Corkscrew Hill. They came from one end of the village and the Connollys on my grandfather's side were on the other side in Loughrask.

As the farming wasn't able to support the person I started giving walking tours for money. Then I studied archaeology because I needed a qualification. Giving the tours is handy because I still have time to get the farming done and the two things kind of complement each other.

I was always interested in Archaeology because around here you're falling over things. Every field you go into there's some archaeological site so it's no harm to know what it is. You'd have an idea anyway as a kid and it's easy to be told things. So you'd have a good curiosity especially if you were told not to touch the tombs or the forts or put your hand in them - then you'd be made more curious; you'd be wondering what's inside since you wouldn't be able to open it up and see what's going on. You might have been told as a child that little people built the forts

- they may have lived there alright but it wasn't they who built them at all. Sometimes they would call something a tomb and another time a Diarmuid and Gráinne bed - they'd both looked the same so you'd be getting mixed messages but would have to go with it. So when you get the qualifications you know what it really is.

You'd be surprised how much the lads around here knew when I was growing up but would never let on, especially about the flowers and things. I know lads who have a great knowledge of that stuff but you'd never think it by them. At that age, they'd be more interested in TV and what's on but they'd be told the same things as me. As you get older, people start to become more interested in things from childhood. My Dad would tell you what things were when you would be passing – through osmosis as much as anything else.

I wish it was sunshine every day here [laughs]. The way farming has gone now you are constantly working against the weather. It's so bad; you only get a few short days to do anything. It's weather, weather, weather and the unpredictability of it is making it very hard to do your work. When I was growing up you could get weeks and weeks where it was fine - and could get something done. We're getting nothing done now and the machinery is getting bigger and bigger every year and it's making a mess of the place. So between the machinery and the weather farming's got very, very hard. And the winter's got longer. My neighbour was telling me he's feeding sileage to cattle for eight months of the year - that's ridiculous - you should only be feeding for four months. I remember starting in January, now we're feeding in October. The cost of that is huge and then there's the cost of the cattle being inside for longer - Between the cattle feeding and us feeling it in the pocket it's a long old winter. And the land has got so wet - like there's rushes where there should be none. And the seasons... like there are no seasons it's just wet and miserable every day.

The machines are gone too big. Somebody that's back from America says that farming in Ireland has gone like farming for the prairies. Those machines work in the middle of Ireland but here most of them won't get in our gates - we have to knock the gate posts to get them in. They're too big and too heavy. They are compressing the soil when they go down the fields and when they turn around they are ploughing it up. Every place is a mess after them.

Before the machines, we had slavery *[laughs]*! There was a lot more labour that time but remember the fields were a lot smaller and it was all done with horses. The problem then was the weather was too dry. I remember my father telling me he used keep swedes for sheep and I thought "Why the hell would he do that?!" But it was because they were wet. You see, the sheep would get moisture from them. That's the funniest thing of all because now the sheep would be up to their neck in muck. They say March and April was too dry with no growth and the summers were longer. It would take maybe a week of fine weather to get the hay done long ago but now you don't get two days of sunshine together to do silage - it's just weather, weather, weather the whole time.

Last year the sheep all got fluke and that's down to the weather - so some people just can't keep sheep anymore. I'm dosing mine every month - they should only be dosed a couple of time a year, that takes money and time. Sometimes the medicine doesn't work because they become immune to it. Fasinex was a big thing for liver fluke but none of us use it anymore because the sheep have all got immune to it - that's serious. Fasinex is made by a big company over in Switzerland. A big company like that should know what they are doing and not allow the weather to have beaten them. There's now something to replace that drug but the sheep will only become immune to it too.

On top of that, you are passing it on to the humans. We're OK, we're honest but there's some people that… You have got to trust the farmer. After giving some medicines you can sell the animal after two weeks but some you can't sell 'til after 56 days because it will make the person sick if they eat the meat before that time's passed. But you have to write down when you dosed them. You might think "I'll remember this; I dosed them today." But come 40 days down the line - it seems like a long time ago. Even with the best of intentions, you could forget if you don't write it down and even if you do you can lose it. And I don't know if farmers are good at record keeping. That wouldn't happen if the weather was any good 'cos you'd only do them a couple of times a year and that would be the end of it.

There's a place for all types of medicine but funny enough if you look into what they put into some of those medicines and you look up the chemical make-up of the plants growing in the fields they probably match what you're paying a fortune for. You'd be surprised how close they are but neither side will say it.

The problem with modern farming is we have a lot more diseases than they had long ago because of the practices we do. I'm just after dealing with a calf that had scour. Very few calves had this long ago because they were outside the whole time - their mother's hadn't too much milk - the cows weren't being pushed with milk. They would be outside the whole time; they were born outside and they stayed outside. The calves today are inside for a week or two then they're let out. So there's that change.

Long ago, also they had a balanced diet. They don't have a balanced diet now - all they have is grass and clover. Before they had more herbs in with the grass. There was less liver fluke then and also if there was land where there was liver fluke they didn't keep sheep there. Now they keep sheep where they shouldn't because they can dose them. In certain places there are floods and turloughs - nobody kept sheep there long ago. So it was about prevention. These days we don't have to prevent because we can always give them a bottle. So we need the modern medicine because farming has changed. They could get away with a lot more long ago because they were preventing it. Or else they weren't doing it, or the big thing was, cattle were outside on a balanced diet.

It's like ourselves - its everything in moderation that's the way

Shane with his father Paddy & mother Mary Jo

the cattle and the sheep were - they're not in moderation now - they're getting 100% grass or 100% silage and then anything they do get is in concentrates and it's like giving them vitamin pills. So it's kind of like we're trying to give them a balanced diet in an artificial sort of a way. That wasn't the way long ago - there was half-a-dozen different plants and half-a-dozen different grasses in each mouthful. But with reseeding you get two or three good grasses and maybe one or two good clovers and that's it. Reseeding is about trying to get the volume or when you're trying to be precise as certain grasses are good for certain things. Long ago the grass was okay but it wasn't great - now we have great grass but there are only a few types - you're dealing with monoculture.

Up the mountain, you would have 30 different grasses and you still have these. On some of the land I would do winterage. But this would be for a shorter time and only a few cattle would be wintered out. The way it has gone here in the Burren - most people would winter out but they'd put up a round feeder with silage in it and then the problem is it gets very messy. The way the winters have gone now; after two days it is pure muck. That's not allowed anymore by the Department of Agriculture so now you have to build slatted houses. And you have to put them in. So you'd have the animals up the hill or at the back of your home so the place would be in muck but it was healthy muck if you know what I mean. But now that's not allowed anymore - you have to have the place pristine. You have to put them into fine big sheds but when you have them in sheds you have to cut silage and to have silage you have to have fertiliser. And then if we put out the slurry, the whole damn lot goes out the one day. But up the mountain you only need a little bit every day - now you have to put it all out on the one day and that's causing pollution. That's the problem - change one little thing and it affects everything down the road. The Department doesn't seem to realise that.

The old people were very good at long-term thinking and long-term planning; they had a broader picture. We don't have a broad picture anymore; it's all about production. And we're forced into it by the crowd that's above in Dublin. The big thing at the moment is cattle prices - you have to have them finished before 30 months. And in all honesty, if you're feeding them on grass you would want 3 years. You can do it on 30 months but they are getting pumped with all the stuff. And you can't have them a long time outside; you have to have them inside in the sheds nice and warm. So we're forced into factory farming. And does the consumer know the difference whether [the animal is alive] 30 months, 31 months or whatever like? But that's what they tell you. This all happened after mad cow disease but when they fixed that problem they should have discontinued it. It was also an excuse for the factory to pay less for the cattle. But now the farmers have all copped on and know to produce in under 30 months so we go with the flow. There are some things they should have scrapped and that's one of them.

Grass-fed cattle would naturally only be ready after three years. We sell our beef that way - we don't sell our beef as factory farmed. With factory farming, you have more slatted sheds, more slurry, and more monocultures. But we've kind of gone into a factory way of things whether we like it or not.

Most factories in Ireland now will not take cattle over 30 months. You have to send cows all the way to the other side of the country (Slaney in Wexford). It's gone that way even with the Quality Assurance Scheme - all this paperwork - the factories slaughter them, bag them, go through the whole vacuum packing process and export them - it's bringing in factory farming. Some things are hard to fix but this is an easy thing to fix. It could be fixed tomorrow morning by getting rid of that rule and it would reduce a lot of the factory farming overnight. But I don't know what the vested interests are at this stage.

You could kill your own animals but you would need a niche market. That's okay but there's 10 million cattle in the country and you won't do them all. The vast majority of farmer's meat is going abroad.

Ah shure, every rule and regulation is… At times you don't blame the English for leaving Europe even though it was stupid; it was the wrong way of fixing the problem. But there's some simple things that could be fixed and they just won't bother. Like the Quality Assurance Scheme - I'm not in that but I know someone who is and he's driven up the wall. Like there's a big exit sign outside the door of his shed - just so in the occasion of fire the cattle know where to go *[laughs]*. He has to have that. I told my brother about it and he couldn't stop laughing - he thought I was only making it up. Just stupid little things like that.

And factory farming is detrimental to the food and to the environment. I know the round feeder is dirty looking; it looks absolutely terrible but the cure, if you think about it, is actually a lot worse. - The slatted house - putting cattle inside especially in these winters and everybody is looking at this big lump of concrete yard you have beyond. So there are umpteen factors that mean that factory farming is not good. The problem with the weather is you are going to have a mess. And people have to understand that if you have cattle, sheep and tractors you can move the feeder around but that can cause a lot of damage too. It can do a fair bit of damage to the archaeology. They should just take it for granted that not every wall you have is going to be up and not every field is going to be clean and once they've got that into their heads you might have some chance.

And now you can't have the cattle near the river. You see this wire going zig-zag and it looks terrible. Shure, there's only a few cattle in these fields anyway and they've been at it for a couple of thousand years so what the hell does it matter if one cow goes into a river?! So now you have this big wire; 'tis like Long Kesh. They are making things too pristine and to have things like that you have to build all these structures. They're thinking about how you keep the river clean and I don't mind keeping the river clean if you have a few thousand cattle there - but for the amount of cattle or sheep that's in the west of Ireland it's crazy. And you'd be afraid to talk to the Department. You'd tell them one thing and they'd go and fix it and then there'd be another problem from that.

Some of the walks that I do have holy wells on the route. The only thing is that often tourists don't appreciate them. The problem is that visually it doesn't look great - it's not a big castle or a big abbey - there are things there you actually cannot see so some tourists get it and some don't. But I'd say they're as important as any castle because the thing about the castle is it's finished; nobody uses most of the castles anymore but the holy wells have been used for thousands of years since there were pagans and are still being used. Of all the archaeology we have the well is the thing that's the longest in use, you know. And it's the religion of the common man too which is quite important. You know when you use the well that your grandmother was doing it and your great-grandmother and they were doing the same things in pagan times. And when you look at the castles and some of the churches - it was only the wealthy that were there but the ordinary man did the wells. And the one thing was that they were for things like the toothaches or the bad eyesight and that kind of joins you up with the person who was there in the stone age. But like a dolmen, good and all as it is it was only really for the special people, the common man was put in a hole in the ground somewhere. Like the tourists all go to these tombs. They were very snobby about these tombs six thousand years ago but being a farmer you would probably not get near a tomb in those times but with the holy well, you can know this is where the common man stood.

My uncle uses the Easter water for the livestock - he goes around the whole farm with it. That's the water blessed by the priest at Easter and left in a big bin in the church porch and you can go in and get it. And there's a place in Galway called Eske and there's water in a holy well there that's for livestock. I don't know is it to do with Saint Martin or somebody but people from here get that for the livestock.

I like the holy wells actually. They span all religions and they're functional. There's something to them but you can't see it and some people appreciate them and some don't. A lot of people travel miles for holy wells. You'd be surprised who you meet and who goes to them. There's a great belief system in them still and it wouldn't be just religious people who use them.

The image that comes to mind most when I'm thinking about the walks is rain, rain, rain, and rain *[laughs]*. You have people saying "God help us! Thank God I'm leaving this bloody country. And I'll be saying "For God's sake, it's a lovely fine day here - don't be complaining!" I had people walking with me a few weeks ago and one of them spent the whole three hours crying *[laughs]*. She was 17 and I think it was a kind of a protest - thanks be to God her parents gave her no sympathy whatsoever. I don't think she wanted to go and she started crying and didn't stop for the whole 3 hours. She got no sympathy - shure that was only making me laugh but thank God I had the parents onside. But I think it was a kind of a protest cry - it was cold and miserable and I said: "This is the way it is the whole time, don't complain."

There are a lot of funny things that happen when I'm out giving the walking tours - I've had everything happen; once, at a holy well I had somebody baptise a child. I don't know what religion they were but the child hadn't been baptised and the grandmother who was on the walk took the opportunity to baptise the child. Holy water, holy well, baby, the grandmother there - you couldn't say no to her. They were American. I think before that the parents said they wouldn't baptise the child but she got the child at the location and it was done. I don't know legally what way it counts but the child got baptised anyway. I think there's something about you not needing to be a priest to baptise a child - an ordinary person can do it in certain circumstances if you have holy water.

I've had proposals of marriage and people scattering ashes on my walks; you'd be surprised what people do. Last year someone proposed above in Black Head - it was a total surprise. I didn't know it was happening - there was no sign of them when I got up to the fort at the top so I went back and he was proposing to her. And other people would come back from America and spread ashes of Irish-Americans in different places.

And sometimes you would be told at the start "I'm pregnant, can we have an easy walk but don't tell the husband I'm pregnant." So we'd be going on this very easy walk *[laughs]* and your man would be wondering "Why the hell are doing this?" *[laughs]*. And why wouldn't they tell the fecking husband and not tell me?! *[laughs]* It would save me a lot of hassle!! And he'd be saying "Shure can we not go up there? I'd rather go up there!!" And I'd be saying "Well we're not going up there; we have to be back." Getting me in trouble! And I'd be thinking "Jesus Christ! She has to tell him sometime. What does a week matter? He might as well know this as next week you know?!" That has happened a fair few times. I don't know why they just don't tell the husband. Or could she not say she has a headache, but she doesn't - she leaves the problem with me.

Tourism in the Burren is going to be good in the future if nobody blows us up. That's the thing - we've a very good image, we're a very safe, secure country. We have a very good image in America and everywhere. I had a man from Japan a few days ago and there's places from America that people are coming from like Idaho and Dakoda - I had a person yesterday from Alabama. Once they only came from New York and Chicago, now they come from all over the States. Oh no, tourism is going to be good; we just have to pray that nobody drops a bomb on us or blows up Dublin 'cos it's easy frighten tourists.

As long as we don't learn to be too clinical either. Like everything has to be 100% according to Bord Fáilte. That's too much. You want a little bit of fun and flexibility - that's what people come to Ireland to see. A lot of people give out about the Cliffs of Moher and the way it has been developed but then "Jesus" I said, "You met me in the church car park and it didn't go five minutes and you were looking for a bathroom." You know, I mean you have to provide services. The tourists have to understand that - there has to be a bit of understanding on both sides. You can't be changing the landscape or changing anything to suit the tourists - the tourists don't want it changed really. Just provide them with the basics and they'll do OK. Some people would be saying "Make this easy for the tourists, make that easy for the tourists." There's no need for that. The tourists will figure it out for themselves. You don't have to give tourists 100% of anything - 90% would do it because

Shane at work on his farm

there's also the cultural things. One time a man told me "God, I went into a shop and the girl working there was grumpy." I said "For hell's sake! That's the Irish girl. What about it?!" You know what I mean?! In America, everybody's 100% polite "Have a nice day." The Irish girl was grumpy. That's the culture - take it and - If you've got a grumpy girl enjoy it.

I was talking to an English man a week ago who was renting a house in Bell Harbour and it had seven bathrooms *[laughs]* and he was giving out about it saying, *"What in the name of God am I going to do with seven bathrooms?"* I said, *"How long are you here for?"* *"Oh, a week."* *"Well then,"* I said, *"that's your answer; can't you use a different one every day?!"* Some people are never happy *[laughs]*.

Siân Morgan
Herbalist based in Kinvara

I met my Irish husband in France as part of my Erasmus year and, after I graduated, moved to Dublin where I studied homeopathy. As soon as the course was over, I decided to get out of Dublin. I didn't really mind where; I just wanted to be in the countryside. My husband got a job in Galway and then we picked Kinvara off a map as a place to live because it was close to the city and looked really nice the way it went around the bay. So, we had never been here and we moved down *[laughs]*. I had worked in health stores in Dublin and was looking for work but nobody had any so in the end, on Valentine's day 2007, I opened my own shop.

After a while we started looking for a house to buy in Kinvara but ended up moving up beyond Eagle's Rock. We had an offer on a house near Kinvara, but we pulled out of the sale because it had a pylon across the road and I started getting really anxious about that. I envisaged myself wearing tin foil hats all the time *[laughs]* and I was like, emailing some woman in America who had done research into electromagnetic radiation who obviously, by her response, thought I was crazy. It had an amazing garden and was in a great location but I just kept thinking that if something happened to the kids which could have been related or totally unrelated I would have always thought, "Maybe it wouldn't have happened if that wasn't there." We just decided it wasn't worth always having that in the back of our minds and pulled out of the sale. The bank had agreed to lend us some money so we had a certain amount of time to look around and then I found our house online. According to my husband, I texted him and said, "I love it, buy it for me *[laughs]*." It's just so peaceful there; so quiet. I love the quiet. If I close my eyes I have a picture of it. D'you know, the location is just so beautiful. I keep turning to the children saying, "You don't understand how lucky you are to grow up here. You will one day but right now you take this for granted because this is what you always have." They certainly find it very loud up in a big city like Dublin. My 6-year-old daughter walks 'round with her hands over her ears because of the noise. And she keeps saying to people, "The only noise by us is cows."

The Burren really feels like home to me which is a strange thing in a way, I suppose, 'cos it's obviously relatively far from home. Yeah... I don't know how to describe that in any other way but I have a real sense of belonging. I had that in Ireland anywhere but very much so, up there.

When I was a kid I moved around a lot between Warwickshire, Hampshire, and France and then went to boarding school. Yeah, I've always been... I'm a real pack animal I guess. Like my husband is forever saying, "Jesus, the amount of clutter!" But it's always been the stuff that I've brought with me that has made a place home but here... Funnily enough, I've been saying to him lately, "We should get a skip and de-clutter." It's home now, I guess, and so I don't need the stuff in the same way.

The very first day I opened - I'd say that most of the people who came through the door were not people born and bred in Kinvara, though that's growing more over the years. Definitely, a lot of people came in on the first day to look around and see what was there and, yeah, shopkeepers from the other shops came to see what was going on; to see who I was and what was happening. Probably most of the customers at the beginning were people who live here but weren't from here. And a good number of them were from Holland and Germany and other countries.

In general terms, I would have said that complementary medicines are more... well, people feel listened to more and the main focus is on holistic health. But I do think that's changing. Like I was just at the local GP this morning and I have to say there is a real sense of being held in this community and even within western medicine as well. But I don't know; I haven't been to a GP any place else for a very long time, so I don't know if that's unique to here. By being held I mean that they really know who everybody is and that you are an important part of the community and are being looked after and heard. Like you can be waiting for hours in that practice but you are waiting that long because they give you the amount of time it takes to hear what you have to say. You're not just a number on a sheet but you are somebody and you matter.

I think a lot of people come into the shop for the chat. Like a talking therapy d'you know. Yeah, we have a lot of people who just come in and... And maybe like the doctors, we try to know people's names and know their children and how they relate to each other. Yeah, maybe there's a sense that it's a place where you can come and be heard. Men do come into us but we probably have more women and often-times the women might come in to get something for their husband or their teenage son.

I wonder how things are here compared to the UK. Like in the UK it's free to go to the GP so you might go to them first, whereas here you may think, 'Shure if I go to the GP it's going to be 50 Euro. Maybe I could see if they have anything in the health food shop instead. We have a code of ethics to our association and we have a protocol for selling herbs and vitamins. So, we can't diagnose an illness and if someone's on medication we can't advise that they take... we can only advise on food and lifestyle changes; we have to be cautious with that.

Not all health food stores in Ireland belong to the Irish Association of Health Stores but we try and get everybody to belong because then we can stand as a professional body. Like, if someone says, "Look, I went to a health-food store and they said it was fine to take whatever thing" we can say, "If you were in one of our member stores we wouldn't have done that because all staff members have to go through this protocol of selling as a bare-minimum training and then there's other training as well. That way it lends more credibility and the stores can bounce questions and information against each other so it's great.

My personal belief is that there's absolutely a need for pharmaceutical medicine; for antibiotics and all those things but very often there is something gentler and more in tune with nature and the body that we could try first. Unless it's… you know, really obviously an acute situation. But for lots of situations, there's something you could try first. I started to be really interested in herbs at boarding school when I was about thirteen and I'm still not sure how I ended up doing homeopathy and not herbalism. But maybe that's the thing; that's what I'm drawn to in the Burren. Like I very much like to be in nature; I like to live in nature and to have countryside around me. That's why I really struggled in Dublin. Much as I'm happy to go and visit my in-laws, I would find

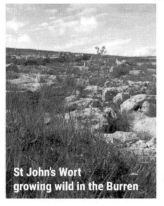

St John's Wort growing wild in the Burren

it really hard to live there again. And even when we did live there I would often have to jump on the DART and go out to the coast. I am very drawn to the sea. So yeah, herbalism is like putting nature inside you and it's that kind of symbiotic thing. I think there's healing in just being in nature and the quiet. With two small children the quiet is something that I have really come to relish quite a lot because there is not a lot

of it *[laughs]*. So yeah, I think it's that thing of being in nature and nature being in you. And I love that in herbal medicine. D'you know like, you could argue that aspirin comes from willow but the whole plant, it contains everything; it's got all the balancing elements. With pharmaceuticals, you've taken out what's deemed to be the active ingredient but there's a reason it was in that plant with all the other stuff. Maybe taking a concentrated extract of something isn't the way the body needs to receive it. I don't know if that makes sense but...

And that idea that if you just use the whole thing... This is totally unscientific and totally out of my head but I wonder if the body just knows how much it needs to use.

Certainly, we wouldn't tend to see side-effects in the same way in plants as in pharmaceuticals. But, I think you do sometimes see side-effects with concentrated extracts. I try not to have them in the shop because I don't think that's the way they're designed to work. That's my personal thing. It's nearly like a medicalised version of a natural product. And they're going that way because they can then say there's x-number of milligrams of active ingredient in a product. Maybe that's to try to get the mainstream more on side: They can say, "Look! We're doing scientific studies too." So there's that pressure out there.

Entrance to Liscannor Holy Well

We're not allowed to make claims on a product unless it's licensed through the HPRA and in order to be licensed it has to have a dossier of information lodged with them.

St John's Wort is now available to be prescribed through a medical herbalist. It was being said that you could not buy here because of European regulations but yet you can buy it in the UK and that happened way before

Brexit.

I don't know much about local healing practices but I go to wells - I'm really drawn to them. I don't go to drink the water, I just like the energy at these places. There is a well near us called St Fachtnan's. I don't know what it's a cure for - I think it might be an eye cure.

I like the idea of the wells as a place where people would congregate and I know that they were holy wells and there were saints attached to them but I like the idea that they were there in pre-Christian times. And the way they would empower people; like they would think "Right! I've got something wrong with my eye so I'm going up to the well in that field." They are putting that trust in themselves to find their own way to healing. And, it might be wishy-washy but the energy up there is really... I know it's all about the science in this world and there's no science to this but I have sometimes been the one in Liscannor and not been able to walk into the tunnel because... I can feel it now - I can feel the hairs on my arms going just from thinking about those times. I wonder if it's just by dint of it being enclosed like that and all the stuff inside but it's nearly like a clamouring; it's nearly a noise that's in there. And what is it? Is it people's hopes and sadness and... I don't know but I find it so intense there. I've brought people to see it and have had to say whispers, "I'm just going to wait here because I can't make it in." Like I can find it quite upsetting there sometimes; it's quite a powerful place.

With regards to the future, being somebody in alternative medicine can feel like not a very safe place to be at the moment. Whilst science is obviously extremely important, it can feel as though, no matter how many studies you can show to support your practice, they are considered insufficient or incomplete - 'bad science'. There is more and more legislation proposed to limit people being able to access their own choices for healthcare and that can feel like a certain degree of nanny-stateism. It can feel like people's power to choose is being taken away - "we know what's best for you so don't worry your head there" By 'we' I guess I mean the mainstream or the government.

To take power of our own healing we need to trust our bodies and ourselves and our intuition more, maybe. I'm a firm believer that there's absolutely a place for western medicine as well, but I think that sometimes we're too fast to say, "I'm going to hand that all over to somebody else." Like, there's a lack of trust in our ability to do things that would have been really natural like childbirth and breastfeeding but yet, you don't get cows not knowing this stuff. Maybe there's a sense that we've handed up so much power in knowing what our bodies do and how they work that we've lost some of those skills as well.

CHAPTER 3
BEYOND THE SOUL

Needles, Pharma Meds & Doing No Harm

"The Doctor of the future will give no medicine but will educate his patients in the care of the human frame, in diet and in the cause and prevention of disease."

Thomas A. Edison (1847-1931) Inventor

In 1815, the enforcement of the Apothecaries' Act required that all medical students wishing to be licensed to practice in England and Wales pass an exam that included a test of herbal knowledge. This marked the beginning of the regulation of the medical profession in Great Britain.

In the 100 years before, there had been a mass importation of cures into the British Isles from as far away as America. In their publication 'Medicinal Plants in Folk Tradition' Allen and Hatfield describe these as "a repository of potential extra weapons in the armoury of learned medicine." Searching close to home in some areas, Allen and

Hatfield tell us, "no longer seemed worth the effort."

However, during the 1800s, several general practitioners in rural Ireland made noteworthy recordings of folk cures. The reason for this may have been purely economic as medicines were expensive and herbs were free but this still demonstrates that, at the time and for at least a generation after, folk cures were respected by the orthodox medical profession.

And so people in Ireland continued folk practices such as visiting holy wells dotted across the Burren in order to remedy minor illnesses such as eye, ear, skin and throat complaints. In addition, they attended healers who could set bones and address liver complaints but who generally knew nothing about surgery. At the same time, industriali-sation in England led to the rampant development of diseases that cried out for new methods and cures and in the 1880s when Louis Pasteur invented ways to prevent bacterial contamination it was hailed as one of the greatest achievements of modern science.

In the Burren of today, as in the wider western world, we have many GPs who are reluctant to dole out prescriptions and who will in-stead recommend acupuncture for back and knee complaints and home cures such as honey, lemon and garlic for minor coughs and colds. And so what is the role of the contemporary practitioner in this world of binaries?

Anne McFarlane
Professor at University of Limerick Medical School

In the early 90's I had finished a degree in Psychology and Sociology in UCC and got a great opportunity to study a Masters with Professor Cecily Kelleher who had established the first Department of Health Promotion in Ireland in University College Galway, as it was then called. Cecily had had discussions with Lelia Doolan about the idea of surveying people's knowledge and use of old Irish folk cures and remedies in the Burren. They had discussed how the old traditions may relate to people's knowledge and use of alternative or complementary medicine as well as modern medicine.

When Cecily mentioned this idea to me I was immediately drawn to the idea. My Dad was a Geographer and had always talked to us at home about the Burren. He made sure we visited the area, walked the limestone rocks, saw the alpine flowers, studied the stalagmites and stalactites in the Aillwee caves and so on. He had a wonderful way of passing on enthusiasm, so I suppose I had this sense of awe in me about the Burren. It was 'an important place'! The other draw for me was that my only sister Lisa, the youngest in our family, had very bad eczema. My parents had spent years visiting doctors and trying out new medications to ease the itching and the pain from sores on her skin. They also gathered information and visited a variety of people and places with other possible treatments and cures. I remember watching Mum pasting a lotion from a small brown bottle on Lisa's little body. It was prepared from plants by a nun in Co. Tipperary. I have a strong memory of collecting goat's milk from a farm and listening to 'conversations of hope' between my Mum and the farmer's wife that this would help.

So, I didn't need a lot of persuading to respond to this research idea. I was interested in the place and the subject matter. The primary aim of the research with Cecily was to explore people's knowledge of and attitudes towards folk medicine, alternative medicine and conventional medicine. We based the study on a nationwide 1930s folklore scheme, which had been carried out by The Folklore Commission of Ireland. What we did involved senior pupils from 11 national schools in the Burren who wrote essays on 'Health Practices.' In total, we collected 133 essays.

In the 1930s study the Burren was found to have a particularly rich tradition of folk medicine and, sixty years on, the pupils from Liscannor, Ballyvaughan, Kilnaboy, Kilfenora, Carron, Corofin, Lisdoonvarna and Kilshanny were delighted to provide us with endless lists of remedies; most of them being for skin, ear, nose and throat aliments. I remember reading that putting garlic in your shoe was a good remedy for a cold, that there were renowned bonesetters in the area and several Holy Wells. There were a lot of references to specific healers and how someone became a healer like was it inherited through a family line or the seventh son of a seventh son or an acquired healing like if a woman married somebody with the same surname then she acquired healing abilities.

Our study also found that the use of folk remedies and folk healers was more likely among people in lower income groups but not by a significant percentage.

In the early '90s, alternative or complementary medicine, as it was becoming known, was booming or coming to the fore in Ireland; becoming more public and more normal. At the time, there was a big health-food shop in the centre of Galway city and just one health-food cafe but when I left Galway twenty years later there was probably ten health-food stores and nearly every second cafe was selling lentils and chickpeas *[laughs]*. I remember there was a big debate about why people were doing this? Like, they had brilliant modern medicine so was it a rejection of this or not? And then a lot of the very good social science research would say it's to do with people being able to navigate between different healthcare systems comfortably. From a biomedical perspective this all looked "wrong" or "illogical" but from an understanding of people's lay health beliefs and what's referred to as their lay-referral systems it had value and validity.

This work, which I was doing as part of my masters led on to a PhD through which we set out to meet older people living in Ireland who would have been in school at the time of the 1930's survey and speak to them about their memories of childhood practices around health and to give us a narrative account of how their healthcare practices changed throughout their life. We conducted about fifty interviews with older people all around Ireland and many of them remembered the original Folklore of Ireland survey happening in their school.

That analysis was interesting because it showed that a lot of people could still remember details of cures, remedies or healing. But, mostly, people had really shifted their allegiance to modern medicine and would rarely engage in folk medicine and weren't particularly interested in alternative or complementary therapies. They saw it as being a better healthcare system and one which they were quite happy to follow.

They would say things like "If my doctor told me to go to acupuncture I would." They were quite loyal to their doctors and to medicine.

The analysis of the older people also showed that when they grew up they didn't go to the doctor because they couldn't afford it or, even if they could, the doctors weren't there and so if they went to one that meant someone was very, very sick. For that reason, the doctor was a very scarce, valued resource. It was that generation raised in the 1930's and 40's that first benefited from the availability of an improved healthcare system that was within easy reach, affordable or even free and which was safer and better than ever before. They would have been the first cohort to benefit from a lot of the key developments in modern medicine like where healthcare was made free to Irish mothers and babies. It is interesting that those who are a generation on and who have had grown up with these benefits are more critical and maybe not so happy with it all.

The other thing we examined was the role of women as health workers both historically and currently. All of the material we had showed that it was women who would know about the options available; women were the carriers of knowledge and wisdom about what your healthcare options were. When you looked at the details of what people knew about folk medicine it was mainly things like "My mother made a poultice" or "my mother knew a healer." And then if you looked at the stories in relation to complimentary medicine and whether older people knew or had tried it, it was often seen to be the role of the daughter or daughter-in-law to say, "There's something you could try" or "This is what I've tried."

I think the way people form their ideas and practices around healthcare has always been rich and complex and shaped by the people and options around them. But the detail of what's maybe around you has changed and the acceptability of certain practices has risen or fallen. This may not apply in the Burren but I wonder if you were in a cafe in Dublin city and you said to someone "I've just been to a faith healer" would you get a different reaction to if you said you'd been to an acupuncturist? I think you might get an eyebrow raised for the first and a clap on the back for the second. That speaks back to the lay referral system; the notion of the repertoire of options available and that people can hold, what look like from a biomedical perspective, contradictory perspectives but they do hold them and they navigate them.

But to me, there is a disparity with complementary and alternative medicine because if you have a medical card or limited income, going into a health food shop can be expensive - and the other main finding is that very few people do it exclusively — most people who are using traditional or complementary medicine are using the treatments to complement their use of the medical system. Also, there's evidence that antibiotics that have been effective for so long are now ceasing to be effective because they've been used too much. There's also a similar discussion around and reaction against the over-medicalisation of depression and the over-use of antidepressants. The evidence seems to be that they these medications do have a place but if they become the first response and are handed out because that's the only thing that's manageable in the ten-minute slot that you have as a general practitioner and they're not embedded into a broader treatment programme; counselling for example, then there is a problem.

I think the rise of chronic conditions is relevant to alternative medicine because the point about chronic conditions is that they're not for curing, they're for living with and so care and management of symptoms and trying to find some sense of progress in that becomes very, very important.

The older generation of people we met had put all their hope in biomedicine and probably experienced a lot of benefit from it but with the rise of chronic disease in Ireland, the nature of the symptoms people now have are different. There's a famous medical anthropologist Arthur Kleinman who has done ground-breaking research on this globally. He writes about different systems of healthcare; the professional sector, the popular sector, and self-care. He talks about how what defines the systems is the extent to which they are regulated and professionalised. For example, in China acupuncture is the professional system but here it isn't. Biomedicine is the professional system and acupuncture would be classified as part of the popular sector. So, he would say that you should look at the level of regulation and professionalisation and that's what positions a practice as being professional or popular in a particular society.

He also says that, across cultures, there are explanatory models. These are based on questions that that people work through in their head to try and understand each illness experience. These questions are very similar no matter what system you're in. For example, they might ask 'what is the symptom, when did it start, how long has it been there and what makes it better?' So, there's a pattern to what the mother will do in the kitchen, what the acupuncturist will do and what the doctor will do. And that is the basis of the challenge to any diminishing of what the layperson is doing because it's actually at quite a high level of sophistication. The use of an explanatory framework to understand symptoms and decide on what to do next is similar across these health care systems and peoples even though your conclusions and actions might be different. That can be very challenging from a biomedical and modern science perspective.

I'm involved in teaching sociology to med' students in the Graduate Entry Medical School, University of Limerick and what I say to the med' students is "Be careful of dismissing patients and their views; take your time figuring out what they think is going on with their symptoms and why they are doing what they are doing. You may not agree with it, you may not advocate it but it is part of their full-health world and you're part of their full-health world and you might as well try to connect and respect each other." This all relates to the difference between what we call reductionism and holism so you could go to an orthopedic surgeon who might analyze your knee but he knows nothing about elbows. Or I remember hearing a story about an ophthalmologist who would focus on the front of your eye and not the back so that is reductionism to the extreme. And then holism is that any symptom or any part of the body is always looked at in relation to the others and to wider life world issues. So, classically complementary medicine looks for the interactions between the symptoms and other parts of your body and other parts of your life whereas, in its extreme form, biomedicine doesn't. It is interesting though that general practice is different in another way because it has a stronger holistic and social-medicine element than, say, surgery would.

That said, I would always be cautious about polarising practices or people because you can have homeopaths who are rushing and GPs who aren't and who put the patient at the centre of the consultation so there is always something about the concept and then the practice.

In our Medical School we have problem-based learning as part of the study programme. What this means is that every week medical students are given the scenario of a person who has a particular problem so as to personalise their medical training.

The name we use in one of these scenarios is David McGrath and in my lecture about the lay referral system I say to the students that we can 'play' around with him to explore health practices. I start by saying let's say David McGrath is living in rural Ireland in the 1900s and so we can look at what his mother can do for him or if he visits the holy well. Then I say we can have him in 2018, living in an urban area but with a father from the country so every now and again he does visit the local well but doesn't tell anyone. We can say David Mc Grath's actually Dimitri and he's a migrant from Russia living in Ireland and look again at his options. Dimitri might be going to the GP but there's no trained interpreter so they don't know what they're saying to each other and [he has to ring home] to talk to someone in Russia.

The point of this is to try to illustrate the stability of those concepts and that they play out very differently depending on who you are, when you are born, what way you're living and is where you live the place you come from.

We're very proud here at UL in that we have a problem-based learning backbone to the curriculum and we begin each year with the examination of a case across a spectrum of disciplines from anatomy, physiology, right through to sociology or law and ethics. So, what we are endeavouring to do is put the person back at the centre of medical education and bring a holistic perspective to how a student is learning about them, their condition and their treatment.

Also, our students here get extended time in primary care; they get about eighteen weeks in general practice attachment which means they meet families in the community, in GP care or in clinics. Traditionally while in med' school the first time you meet a patient is when they're in hospital in their pyjamas. Our students get to visualise them in their identities as 'full people' rather than being reduced to a sick patient.

From the early 60s and 70's in GP practice, there has, conceptually, always been an emphasis on how important the patient is as well as their family and community.

Maccon MacNamara
Retired General Medical
Practitioner from Corofin

My great-grandmother was one of the Unthanks, a Quaker from Limerick. When my great-grandfather and her came to Corofin in 1826 he set up a general practitioners which stayed in our family for four generations. When I began practicing in '66 the surgery was really Dickensian. One day, I saw a tourist taking photographs of it and realised it was time to do something. All I had was cold water, a toilet, a bucket and a big, huge turf fire. And so, I set up a surgery at home and eventually built the bungalow in the town.

In those times, I was a one-man band. I had no nurse and no secretary; no one to answer the phone, I was on call 24/7. And when I'd go in there'd be eighty-year-olds struggling to get up out of their seats to say, "Good morning, doctor." I'd feel like a right clown but one day there was a man just sitting lighting his pipe and he said, "Soft day Maccon." My cover was blown *[laughs]* and after that, there was nobody jumping to attention when I came in which pleased me no end.

The patients then were fantastic - I looked after all the old people and when I look back on it, that was such a privilege; you visited them in their houses, you knew everything about them - if you got a call to house 'X' you knew there was something wrong and you had better go straight away but if you got a call to house 'Y' you could wait a fortnight before you went down. I remember some patients who were asthmatics and I'd say, "Why didn't you call me in the middle of the night?" and they'd say, "We didn't like to disturb you, doctor." These days they'd say, "Get your ass down here now or we'll report you to the authorities." I'm not computer literate or anything like that but I would regard medicine then as an art and now it's an exact science.

Before I qualified, I used to have to assist my father at post-mortems in the patient's houses which was horrific - you'd have the relatives out in the kitchen maybe crying or drunk and you'd be in the bedroom doing the post mortem. Like a GP doing a post mortem in the patient's house was a joke from a medical point of view. I think my father had a razor blade, he would make an incision in the patient's chest and then sew it up again and say, "Heart attack." There were no pathologists around at the time except if it was a murder or something like that. The amount of people it was said died of a heart attack when we hadn't a clue what it was but it helped with statistics at the time.

I had four standard potions; a cough bottle which my grandfather made and patients swore by it. Then there was one for the stomach; an antacid; one for constipation and diarrhoea; and a tonic - syrup of figs. I got the ingredients from the health board. I would mix them together myself. None of these ingredients are available now if you went into a chemist shop. My father used get a locum in and every morning he'd come into the surgery and say, "Hands up for cough bottles." Nowadays there's about two-thousand cough bottles on the market but taking them can be a complete waste of time.

Different doctors had their ways in those times. I remember one who was tough as nails; it was said he'd get by on three hours sleep a night a night. I once heard a story about him coming down to the waiting room of a morning - he has a vicious hangover and he says, "I can't get through this." So, he goes into the surgery gets the fiddle comes back to the patients and says, "We'll have a half session inside in the surgery." So, a whole pile of them get up to dance and he looks at them and says, "You can go home and come back tomorrow." And I remember hearing that if he didn't have a stethoscope he'd put half-crown on their back and say, "Breathe in, breathe out" and nobody'd be any the wiser.

Pharmacology was in its infancy to an extent when I was starting out. We had sleeping tablets, but they were just barbiturates. God! If you gave that much barbiturates today you'd be struck off in a very short time. And there was very little sedation; there was no Xanax. Libactyl probably changed the face of psychiatry to some extent and it was one of the first drugs that was released without any trials at all. There were quite a fair bit of psychotic patients back then around the place, they had to be got by the Gardaí or a grab team would come out from Galway and take them to the mental hospital. Like they would be a danger to themselves in ways. And suicide was present. One of the worst tasks I ever had was cutting the rope and trying to catch the body.

Fortunately, with psychiatry now there isn't as much of that. Though with suicide there is a lot with young people with drugs and stress and the inability to cope, not having enough money or housing or things like that. In those days everyone emigrated; if a farmer had eight children the eldest got the farm and the rest had to do a runner elsewhere. In the '40s there was a huge amount of emigration and it was terribly sad seeing people heading off with a cardboard suitcase and a shovel to Birmingham. And when they got from Corofin to Birmingham there'd be signs up saying 'No blacks, no Irish.' Where I went to primary school only two girls and two boys went on to university but nowadays everyone goes to university. Back then you had the choice of the civil service, the banks or picking up a shovel.

The patients could be very witty people as well. They weren't as demanding as people are today. I'm twelve years retired now but I talk to colleagues and they say they're demented with people demanding things like MRIs or CAT scans because someone said it would be good for diagnosis. And they want the result half an hour later and are ringing at 9 or 10 o'clock at night saying, "Did the results of my blood test come back today?" or whatever. A lot of the older GPs can't wait to retire. And all the book work... Like I had hardly any book work - I kept my notes to the very minimum particularly if it was something very personal, I would just write down 'Advised' on the chart so there would never be queries about it. Occasionally I'd write down FAW - if I had to explain to the judge what FAW was I'd say "F*?! all wrong [laughs]." You might get people coming back all the time and there was nothing wrong with them and you'd get a bit peed off. Like, if you were on call all the time you could be driven up the wall by someone say calling you at three in the morning for a pain in the big toe or something like that.

My father once told me about an incidence in the days before electricity where a lady had a retained placenta. Paraffin oil was scarce at the time and they had to get a doctor in Ennistymon to give the aesthetic using ether. The only source of light was a box of matches and there was a danger they'd blow the house to pieces. Another time, they were delivering a baby and again there was no light and so they had to use a bicycle lamp. On the way home, the midwife said to my father "Wasn't it lucky they had the bicycle lamp, otherwise the husband would have had to bring in the bicycle with the dynamo and imagine the scene with him cycling away at the end of the bed?!"

I'm a survivor - I've have had four different bouts of cancer in my lifetime, I don't know how I survived them - how or why. I've never had radiotherapy or chemotherapy for any of them. My first operation was by a GP in Limerick when I was eleven; they took out my appendix. They used open ether; the mask on your face and slosh bottle, you'd try not to breathe 'cos it tasted horrible. I remember I was allowed out of bed on the 10th day afterwards which was absolutely revolutionary; usually, they were kept in for a fortnight - now you'd be home two days later.

During my training, when I was employed in a hospital you did a full physical examination on a patient; even if you came in with an ingrown toenail every system was gone through SNS, respiratory system recorded and reflexes. Today, you could easily miss something in pathology. Like if a patient comes in with condition 1 very often there would be condition 2 there as well. Everything is done now; CT scans and MRIs. It was very hard even to get an X-ray back in those days and there were very few blood tests being done.

There's too much attention to hygiene these days. Nature can cure a lot if left alone; we need to build up resistance. My father used to say, "A dirty child is a healthy child." I do believe that 'cos nowadays they are off to the doctor with the slightest drip from the nose demanding antibiotics. We are prescribing miles too much antibiotics and we are sort of forced into it. That's why hospitals are the most dangerous places you could possibly go to. I had a very bad malignant melanoma in my leg. I was 73 and that leg hadn't seen the sun for about 50 years, but I had it anyway. I'd qualified and trained in Galway and was in plan 'C' in the VHI and so was expecting red-carpet treatment but when I got there I was on a trolley for seventeen hours and within three years I was MRSA positive; I'd picked it up in the hospital. And so, I was on a massive dose of antibiotics for a month.

To any young doctors starting out, I'd say "Listen to the patients." If it's a mother with a child they might talk ráméis (rubbish) for the first ten minutes but let them take their time and listen. I didn't have an appointment system in my surgery because patient 'A' might take two minutes and patient 'B' might take 35 minutes. It worked out well that way for me. Nowadays its ten minutes and you could only mention one condition - if you had another you would have to come back again. I'm quite proud of being old-fashioned in a lot of ways. But there's so many expectations and so many tests being done. Fortunately, I got through my life without being litigated but it is fearful for doctors because if you are accused of neglecting somebody and word would go round, it could drag on for two years before an official decision was taken. And then the thing might be dismissed but in the meantime, the doctor's reputation could be ruined. The Medical Council, who decide if someone's guilty or not guilty, has more lay people than doctors on it. Very often people are anti-doctor and think they need to be put in their place and that's why so many tests are done that are totally unnecessary. In obstetrics now if the baby isn't born 100% it's the doctor's fault no matter what happens. And the HSE then fights everything to the last minute and delays things. If the patient dies in the meantime like if they have cerebral palsy the family will get no money but if the case goes on until he's ten or eleven the parents will get millions. So, if I wanted to set up as a private obstetrician I'd have to pay nearly 500k a year in insurance. And insurance is just going up and up and up and up.

There were eight health boards in the country once, then the government decided to have the HSE and all the health boards had to be joined. Nobody was to lose their job as part of this, so you have eight managers and eight assistant managers. When doctors ring for an opinion they'll be passed on through the system and can't get an answer because there are so many managers crawling over one another. When I set up, it was the county manager, his assistant and an accountant that ran the health service in Clare and it worked.

Everything is centralised now as well - In my time if there was an emergency here, I'd ring the ambulance and say, "Can you come out as quick as you can?" and they'd ask, "Where are you?" And I'd say, "You know beside Johnny's house and past the hayshed that's burned down?" and they'd answer, "Oh yeah, we'll be out straight away." But now it's in Athlone. Like they might not even know where Corofin is.

I wouldn't wish medicine on my worst enemy today. The people going into it are the brainiest and brightest but to be a good GP you have to understand people and listen to them, you don't need to know that much medicine in fact. You have all these square pegs in round holes now. An awful lot of them are emigrating because they're highly qualified and they are welcomed all over the world with better working conditions and better back up facilities, income and lifestyle.

Medicine comes from natural sources but when it comes to alternative practices, the first thing that comes to mind is 'do no harm.' I've an open mind though I don't know much about in faith healing.

There wasn't much herbalism around in my time. Though my wife's mother was a nurse and she used quite a bit of folk medicine - cobwebs for bleeding and dock leaves and all that.

You have a lot of Chinese places in Ireland now. Even in Ennis, I think there's two that do herbalism. I know nothing about them so I'm not for them or against them; as long as they do no harm that's okay. I'm on an antibiotic at the moment - I have to be on it for the next 10 days. I have to say, I looked up the notes last night and saw the side effects - Oh Jesus! *[laughs]*. If you put a patient on something and you have to tell them "These are the potential things that can go wrong with it..." Like with the one I'm on a side effect is that my Achilles tendon could snap - and that's just one of its side effects.

So, it's about do no harm, look at what you're taking and that it's not going to damage you. As a doctor, listen and look at your patient as a whole person; be holistic if you want to take herbs but if you need antibiotics; face it.

I typed up some anecdotes that I picked up from patients and other doctors - one doctor from Tipperary was out cycling on the road and was knocked down when a woman walked out in front of him and he said: "God damn you, you old fool!" And she said, "And God bless you doctor - and may neither of our prayers be heard *[laughs]*".

Liam with his mother Mary

Dr. Liam Glynn
Practicing GP and Lecturer based in Ballyvaughan

"Wherever the art of medicine is loved, there is also a love of humanity."
Hippocrates

My family comes from around Tubber and so growing up I'd have heard stories about the Curtis's, Biddy Early, Gerry Donoghue and individuals like that. They'd have been very highly regarded in terms of their ability to cure certain human and animal ailments.

But, I suppose both my grandmother and my mother would have been very focused on things like a good, natural diet and the availability of particular plant cures. Like things as simple as the dock leaf for nettle stings, hot milk and honey for when had a cough and boiled milk for diarrhea.

Every morning on our way to school we'd be sent in over the

wall to pick wild garlic when it was in season and chew it on the way as a preventative for colds and flu. Of course, it didn't make us that popular in school that we smelled of garlic the whole time *[laughs]* but it seemed to work because we were never sick.

So that was a natural thing and in terms of my own journey - that was very much part of it but then I decided to do medicine. And there's no doubt that it was probably influenced by that because I was interested in people and in healing, though in a very general sense. I certainly wouldn't say I said to myself "Oh, I really want to be a doctor." It wasn't like that. I certainly ruled out everything else and put four universities for medicine and one for forestry and wildlife down on my CAO forms. I suppose, that's probably telling of itself in terms of my interest in nature.

For me, I started my education in something that's very effective in some areas but has quite a limited approach to healing and I suppose that dualism has been a constant theme throughout my career in terms of working with people who are ill. But I don't see it as a conflict; a lot of people do and adopt very fundamentalist positions where it's either one or the other. I'm not like that; I really do think the two can work together because, for example, if you come into me with septicemia, you can take all the garlic you want but what you need is IV antibiotics. So, there are very clear areas that formal medicine is good at, there are also very clear areas that it's poor at and then there's a bit of grey in between where you can be unsure as to which is the most effective or whether you should try things together in terms of - let's call it a traditional medical approach versus an alternative or complementary approach - there are lots of different terminologies so I'm not even sure of that myself. But my background would certainly make me open to that type of thing and I'm glad to see that there's an emerging scientific evidence base for some of these - what are regarded as alternative therapies such as acupuncture and homeopathy. Some people adopt really negative approaches towards homeopathy; there are randomised controlled clinical trials which are the highest form of research evidence showing homeopathy works but still, there are loads of sceptics out there.

There's a lot of conflict but not from me personally because I think all of these things can help. I'm open-minded but not so open that my brain falls out. I do like to be rigorous in my approach to stuff and have some evidence base but I'm also really aware of the power of the placebo effect. If you come into me and you're ill and I sit down and you perceive that I care about you and that I'll try my best for you and that I'll listen and spend time with you; if I do all those things, then you're going to feel better no matter what the condition is. This idea of the healer as the drug is an interesting one. We would say "the doctor as the drug" in medicine because that's a well-recognised phenomenon too - there are loads of different things at play.

The most important thing we do is communication. I always say to the students who come here "That's the skill which I really want you to go away with. I want you to work on your communication skills, your empathy, your appreciation for the context that people live in." We well know that formal medical education normally leads to decreased levels of empathy and decreased levels of professionalism around communication skills so there's something we're doing in medical schools that isn't right. But I think a lot more medical educators are recognising that. I'm really delighted that the medical school I work in has such a strong community-based element to education. We're totally unique; most universities in the country have 2-4 weeks of general practice placement; we have eighteen weeks. And it all depends on their mentors and teachers but certainly our students get more of an ability to develop those areas which are very important and outside of just what to prescribe and when.

Even though things are pressured here at times, being in the countryside means we definitely have a little bit more flexibility from the point of view of the amount of time spent with each doctor. I know our patient population by and large are incredibly appreciative and a lot of them are very self-sufficient in terms of their own health. Often they will try self-management first; they'll try a bit of paracetamol or stuff they know or they might even go to an alternative practitioner because there are lots of them available here in the Burren so I think people are much more open to that type of thing.

With regards to traditional medicine, faith healing and alternative medicine, I work within one of those, what you might call, silos. But, of course, they cross over because people would know I'm open to things outside and would discuss this with me sometimes. They're also very aware of GPs or doctors who would be completely not open so they wouldn't have those conversations. But still, for a lot of people, they don't disclose to me that they've been to a faith healer or alternative practitioner because they think I might frown upon it. But I think there are cohorts of people depending on their age, context, tradition, belief systems, health-seeking behaviour and all these different factors who do things in a certain order or who use particular alternatives or combinations of alternatives. So I'm not sure you can be too generalisable about that.

Most alternative practices are relatively newly available here. The older generation wouldn't have been exposed to them when they were young and so probably wouldn't trust them. They would have been exposed to faith healers when they were young and probably would have some level of trust or not, as the case may be, depending on their experiences. I can certainly see that older population maybe not using alternative medicine but using a combination of faith healers and traditional medicine. The people who use alternative medicine certainly seem to be more of a middle-aged or younger population who are more familiar with it and have enough insight to go and investigate themselves and make a decision. This is opposed to having a, maybe, paternalistic approach to healthcare as in leaving it up to their practitioner to make all the decisions which, I suppose, the older generation is content to do a bit. They often don't want an explanation about what's going on; they don't want to have a big conversation, they just want to come in and get treated. And a lot of that is based around fear and stuff like that too.

I heard a story so many times when I was young from my grandmother about a local man with TB who returned from America to die and was nursed back to health. She would have always said it was the sea and mountain air that cured him because they used to take him out in the horse and cart for trips every day to get him the fresh air. Where we lived wasn't that far inland and you'd almost smell the sea at times - even though I think half of that was in our imagination. So, I suppose that was a great story in terms of healing but, of course, if you're being skeptical about it or playing devil's advocate then you would say some people have immunity that allows them to survive TB. But it's around stories like this that healing traditions and practices are built.

If you look at it from a formal medicine point of view you're extrapolating one experience to a whole population which may not work and that's why the idea of having a thing called a randomised control trial is good. In this you have a hundred people who you divide into two groups; half of them get the treatment and half of them get something that looks like the treatment so everybody thinks 's they're getting the same. So that's the whole idea. But yet that structure also has great limitations. We know that now because as a GP you're making a decision based on the people who went through that trial and they might not be at all like the person who's sitting in front of you.

Mary Glynn
Mother and Faith Holder from Tubber

I had a friend, Fr. David, who suffered many illnesses during his lifetime. He was a missionary priest who spent many years in Africa. Despite all his ill health, he was one of the most joyful and loving people I have ever known. Leon Bloy, the French novelist and poet, wrote that "Joy is the most infallible sign of God's presence" , and according to Thomas Aquinas "No man has joy unless he lives in love." Fr. David exuded both and touched everyone he met with that joy and love.

I once read that we "dare not get rid of our pain before we have learned what it had to teach us". Fr. David learned a great deal from his pain, getting many insights into suffering and healing during his illnesses and I was privileged that he shared them with me. On one occasion when he had developed secondary bone cancer and was deemed to be terminally ill by his doctors, much to their astonishment, he made a remarkable recovery and went on to live to a ripe old age. He felt very deeply at the time that it was all the love, good wishes and prayers which came to him from around the world that ultimately brought his healing. He could feel the power of this love and prayer reaching him and explained it as follows: When we reach out to another human being with loving concern and prayer, we become channels for God's healing love to flow through us to that person.

Prayer is a form of intention and "intention" is recognised as a subtle form of energy transference in the laws of physics. In this instance, I believe, we are tapping in to the healing power of a "universal" energy, the source of which is the Divine, becoming conduits of that energy for one another. Teilhard de Chardin, the famous Jesuit priest and scientist has written extensively on this matter, describing the profound oneness of all the elements of the Universe held together by this energy which connects us all to each other, to nature and to God. Every day of our lives we have experiences of this connection, for example when we meet a joyful person our spirits are lifted and when we meet a gloomy person our spirits are dampened. Likewise with nature, when we see a beautiful sunset or behold a beautiful scene we are deeply moved. When the new life of Spring bursts forth from the earth, new life stirs in our hearts too. We feel more alive, our bodies feel lighter and we can actually feel the 'Spring' in our step. The author Daniel J. O'Leary aptly describes it as follows "The heartbeat of every living thing beats in our hearts too and they all beat in the heart of God".

Fr. David's experience became very real for me during my own cancer journey in 1989. I too at all times could feel the power of this love, good wishes and prayers coming to me from family and friends and it really did help to carry me through. I also experienced some very uplifting serendipitous moments which left me in no doubt that I was not alone on this journey. For example, I was recommended two books to read which were "Love, Medicine and Miracles" and "Peace, Love and Healing" both by Dr. Bernie Siegel the renowned cancer specialist.

I had intended ordering them, but a few days later I found them on my doorstep. Only later did I discover who the kind donor was.

I also learned that when we get cancer or any other serious illness we are taken on two journeys. The first journey is the outer or physical journey. After the shock of the diagnosis, there are the appointments with doctors, hospitalisation and treatment which can all be traumatic and challenging. The second or inner journey is an equally important one where hopefully we can find healing for our often troubled hearts and minds. What affects the mind affects the body. When we become ill, of necessity the momentum of our lives change. We have to take time out from our busy lives and retreat into a quieter space where we begin to pay more attention to our inner life. We become more open, more aware and more receptive so more likely to seek the help we need to begin our path to inner healing. I have found meditation to be a very helpful tool. First of all it aids the release of stress which can underlie a lot of health problems. It also brings us to a place of deep rest and relaxation for both body and mind which contributes greatly to the healing process. According to the poet Rainer Maria Rilke, "My looking ripens things as they come towards me to meet and be met." We, perhaps for the first time begin to glimpse our true selves and begin to connect into the deep peace and harmony and that store of love that lies at the core of our being. Whether we realise it or not all human nature longs for this connection. We start to live more mindfully in a more positive and loving frame of mind, not allowing our fears and anxieties to dominate our lives. We develop a much greater awareness of the wonder and beauty of the world around us and a deeper sense of gratitude for all the blessings in our lives and perhaps even for the illness that brought us to this point. I have come to believe through what I have learned from others, and from my own experience, that we can all be channels of healing for one another by connecting into the Divine energy of the Universe through our love, concern and prayer for each other. The challenge for all of us is to be that loving, caring and healing presence in our hurting world.

At Blackhead

CHAPTER 4
BETWEEN SKY, LAND & SEA

Nature as Nurture

In 1925, Alfred Watkins, a self-taught amateur archaeologist, antiquarian and businessman published 'The Old Straight Track' in which he coins the term 'ley lines' which he describes as "surveyed alignments articulated to the prehistoric landscape and movement through it". Whilst this book is based on studies of his native Herefordshire, the search for ley lines became a form of cult in years to follow as ley hunters devised grid paths the width and breath of Europe, many relating to pre and early Christian structures.

Whilst there can be no clear evidence as to the spiritual significance of these leys, many of us report feeling a sense of magic when walking these ancient paths once traversed by pre-Christian and Christian druids, saints, monks, farmers and tradespeople. Whether this is due to the knowledge and vast archaeological evidence of what has passed here since the Stone Age, the sheer beauty of many of the routes, or the spirits who linger matters little as long as our focus is to nurture and protect these priceless remnants of shared history. The Burren is said to contain many leys, though their location is still up for debate. One pleasant way to spend a rainy afternoon is to speculate the placements of the early churches, megalithic sites and marker stones drawn out on Tim Robinson's acclaimed map of the area. One such line could be drawn from St Colmán MacDuagh's hermitage in The Burren National Park, to the three churches of Uchtmáma and on to Corcomroe. Whatever your beliefs, you'd be hard pressed not to get a sense of wonder and magic from this place with its whistling stone walls, lakes that spring from sinkholes in the wintertime, precipices, caves and erratics of granite rock swept over from Connemara during the Ice Age. The gentle bays, rugged shale cliffs and karst landscape made many millions years ago from an accumulation of sea shells and fish bones bring us a sense of being in a different universe from the fast-paced technological world of cities and towns.

As a recent convert to all-year-round sea swimming, my breath is often taken away by the sheer beauty and delight of bringing my head above water and opening my eyes to see the stony-grey hills curving around the bay and the openness of the sea leading across to Galway whilst the cormorants duck and dive just feet away and the occasional seal watches us from a distance. My blood doesn't come from this land but like most already here, I feel a protectiveness and desire to nurture this environment that's been allowed to stay true to itself through industrial revolution, war, famine and more recent technological advances. This is a place where we can sense the ghosts of the past, study their history, celebrate their many layers of worship but be grounded in a present that feeds our bodies, minds and spirits from its good soil, clean air and invigorating sea.

Tom Kelly
Retiree and labyrinth
owner based in
Gleninagh

I lived in Galway for a while and for some reason when we would go for a drive, we'd tend to come this way rather than Connemara. There was always that interest in the Burren and we kept coming back every year. Maybe 25 years ago my son, wife, daughter and I were over Gussy Deely's side and we saw a path coming over the hill and we didn't know where it led. My wife and daughter weren't into walking, but my son and I walked over and came down to where I live now The house wasn't on the market then but ten years later, we were passing and saw the for-sale sign and bought it. It wasn't in a great state - the ceilings were black. I remember when I told a friend of ours, we'd bought it they said "Jaysus! What are you going to do with that place - knock it?!" And he told everyone I'd bought this shack in the Burren. But it was the location - I wanted somewhere by the sea.

I'm originally from Clones in Monaghan - right on the border where people would be very conscious of which side you were on - whose who, what shops you went into and all of that - without anything being said but it was understood all the time. My then wife could never understand when we'd go up there and I'd say, "Oh watch that fellah." There'd be all these nuances - she came from Roscommon where there were no differences between anybody, and you weren't watching out for religion or differences like that. So that's where I grew up and that definitely has an impact on you - in that you're more - what would I call it? You're more cautious with people.

When I was growing up in Clones, they used to say there's two types of people - smugglers and informers. And you'd be very conscious to say nothing - say nothing and keep on saying it. You'd be very suspicious of anyone coming round asking you questions. So probably people say about me that I wouldn't be as open as many people would - it's what you've been with and what you grew up with.

One thing that really amazed me here was the welcome and the openness. There are so many people here with alternative lifestyles. I used to live in Dublin - I left in '95 but I'm still up and down a bit. But I would know far more gay people in Ballyvaughan than in Dublin. Obviously, things in Ballyvaughan have become more open but one of the things I like is how people can live various alternative lifestyles. Now maybe I'm not part of the inner sanctum of the community but I've never heard anything negative or any adverse comments about the lifestyles people have chosen. That's one thing I really like - the acceptance of difference in whatever way it is. Now there's still the instilled sense of being a blow in or whatever. But I got a compliment the other day when I was asked if I was a local or a blow in and someone commented "No, he's somebody who lives locally." A step up above the blow in. That's what I like - the small things.

When we bought this house I was working in Dublin and was under a lot of pressure and stress. I worked at a bank [called Anglo Irish] that's well known for all the wrong reasons and there were certain things I wasn't prepared to do and that was stressful. One thing I noticed is that when I came down here for the weekend - when I'd cross the Shannon things would start to lift and then coming down here - things eased. It just felt like that maybe because you were leaving Dublin behind you. But also, I saw the lifestyle here. We were doing quite well in Dublin but here I saw people who were on a fraction of what I was earning and had a better quality of life.

When Mick Carrucan was alive, I'd go into his house and I loved to hear his old stories. He'd be talking about the fairies and the sí gaoithe - the fairie wind that would come in a hayfield and it would twist around like a mini tornado and it would turn the hay around and lift it up. Mick's wife would say "Oh, stop talking about that!" She didn't like these things. But years ago I was in hospital and I had a heart procedure and had to spend a night or two and when I came home there was a plastic bag hanging on the door that contained a pint of milk, a pizza and a sandwich. Chris Carrucan who was in her 80's had cycled the three miles to my house, hung it and cycled back home. She had serious health problems as well at the time. So there's that sense of belonging and community as well.

There was one farmer who had a potato field down here. I met him in the pub one night and we were just talking about general things and his field and how his potatoes were and whatever. Two days later a bag of potatoes was left at the door. Now I didn't ask, and he didn't say but he just left them.

I've always had an interest in history and archaeology and things like that but how the labyrinth came about was that maybe 15 years ago there was a woman called Bridín Twist who had a centre round the other side of Mullaghmór. It was one of those places you could go for retreats or if you were into Reiki or some kind of alternative thing - people would give talks there. There was going to be a woman giving a talk on NLP (Neuro-Linguistic Programming) that I heard about and one of the guys that developed it - a guy called Bandler had lived here in Ballyvaughan for a few years. I was interested in the idea of how words could influence people and, to be honest, I was interested in it business wise - like how could I make you buy my widgets. So anyway, this weekend was organised over there, and I went to it though, to me, it was nothing about NLP at all - it was a relaxing weekend and just about bringing things from within yourself out and talking about it and I think

I'd just recently separated at that stage. So it was about that and people talking about their experiences. It bothered me that we were just there for a weekend as one or two people had obviously gone through pretty horrendous difficulties and maybe I was wrong but there was an impression that if you came here for the weekend you could leave all your difficulties aside and go away. There was one woman in particular and I felt we were deserting her on the Sunday evening - we had opened it up and not closed it. That part of it bothered me.

Anyway, Brídin Twist had a labyrinth on her grounds which was much bigger than the one I have now and the first thing the facilitator said was "I want you to get in pairs and one person blindfolds the other and the other person is to lead them through." So there was this woman and we were at the top and I was to blindfold her. And I knew immediately she was really tense and bothered by this. She told her story afterwards which was amazing. I think she was a single mother - she was living in the Northside of Dublin and one day she saw a course in the Southside that was into healing or something like that, but it had started the week before. She went over and met the guy and said "This is for me. I really want to do this." But he said "It's started. You've missed the deadline, There's a waiting list and there's no way you can do it." But she persevered and she got on it. And then on the way back home she thought she had to pay for it - she had no money, so she put an ad' up in Trinity to get a student in and then went to a friend of hers to say, "You have to mind my child." But just what amazed me was the determination of her to get what she wanted — somebody who had an idea and the way she followed it through. So when I blindfolded her it was the first time in years, she'd ever given up control and the idea was that I had to lead her round the labyrinth blindfolded and stop and just feel the earth and feel the stone. We did that and when we got to the centre there was this strong feeling like an energy, and I don't know what it was - physical energy or mental energy or a combination and I said to her 'Did you feel something when we got to the middle of it?" And she said "Yeah" and so that started my interest in labyrinths.

The next day we were doing the labyrinth again and the facilitator said: "OK, this time I want to walk it on your own." I asked, "Are you going to blindfold us again?" And she said, "No, no, no, just do it at your own pace." I was first in the line and I thought "Well if we did it blindfold-ed, I wonder what it would be like to do it with my eyes closed." I didn't have them closed the whole way round. I just walked and the others were saying "How's he walking this way?" And they started.

So anyway, when we bought this house there was a big empty space up there and I was lazy in terms of gardening so that's how I made the labyrinth.

There are different people that have walked it and have had different experiences. One guy won the lotto 3 times. Another friend of mine she was doing some exams online and the online system collapsed, and she failed the exam and had to repeat it but if she didn't pass the second exam she was out of the course. Now she did a lot of study as well but then she came up and walked the labyrinth and got 88% in her exam. Obviously, I'm putting it down to the labyrinth but there's a lot more in it than that *[laughs]*. There's a guy here in the village - a very interesting man and he's into all these ley lines and he was saying that there's an energy line coming down this driveway. I'm not convinced by the ley line thing - I'd be very skeptical - maybe I'd been christened Tom 'cos I'm a doubting Thomas. But I saw where in the UK they were able to find that there's one particular entity and they had all these places over the UK and the ley lines could all join up with it - Woolworths stores. Basically, if you take two points you can join them up from A to B.

Anyway, Dominic was the guy who researched what type of labyrinth would fit here best. The one that was researched was based on Chartres Cathedral in France outside Paris somewhere. It's based on the floor of it. A mathematician has studied the geometry of Chartres from a purely mathematical point of view and they seem to have used pure mathematics to build it in a certain way and some would say that this ancient maths is found deep in nature as well - in mathematical dimensions. I only know a little bit about it, but they find these mathematical dimensions in certain plants and shells.

The guys who built it were asking me where I wanted the entrance and I said: "Shure, I don't know" and just picked that point up there. Dominic followed the line of the entrance around the world and it brought him to Machu Picchu where I went walking last year. Now he would claim it's also lined up with Tara and all that sort of thing, but he's been gone now a few years.

Tom's Labyrinth

They built labyrinths in certain hospitals in the US for people who were suffering from Alzheimer's or Dementia. It seems that the walk and the turning from left to right, the brain throws some sort of switch that it helps them relax and get some relief. Now they're not curing it and it doesn't last that long but there's some evidence that simply walking it and that process of turning calms the brain or whatever.

And there's also the idea that I tell my grandkids. "Your goal is to reach the centre and when you start off, you're very near it and other times you're far away." I've a video of the kids running round it - six of them - and it looks totally chaos. But sometimes when it looks like you are going the wrong way or other people are ahead of you or behind you you've got to keep going. It's the lesson of life and that's what I'm saying to them.

Labyrinths are in Celtic traditions as well. They found them in drawings and paintings. They're also in Greek mythology with the Minotaur (half man half beast – dwelling at labyrinth centre) and all of that and then it was adapted to Christianity and some would say the labyrinth was used by the poor people as their journey to Jerusalem. They couldn't afford a pilgrimage to Jerusalem, so this was their way of going there - a purely symbolic way.

People say to get the best out of it you should relax beforehand or meditate which I always find very hard to do. Or some would say if there's something on your mind just say, "Well, I'm thinking about this issue or this question." and walk with it in your mind. Some would say it might lift a bit or maybe you would get an answer. There's all sorts of different ideas like walking in to go somewhere and then walking out away from wherever you were and looking back and reflecting as you're coming out. But it's something I know very little about and I keep saying I must learn more.

What I'd like to see is people using it. Some find it very relaxing. My sister was down here with a bus group from Dublin and about 40 walked it and thought it was fantastic. Others walked it and it means nothing. But that's a bit like the Burren. I have a few people I know that can't understand what I'm doing here. Like a cousin of mine in Belfast can't understand what I'm doing here when I'm single and free and have no ties anywhere and could be out 'enjoying myself' as he would see it. And he'd tell people I'm living in this wilderness and he just doesn't get it at all. And there's a few other people that don't get it and I think that's great because what I'd be afraid of - if everybody got the Burren like they get Killarney we'd be overrun.

To be honest, watching the buses coming up and down bothers me to the point that I shouldn't get annoyed but yet I do. Literally, people driving along and taking a photograph. I'd love to say, "Would you ever just get out of that car, walk even 100 yards and tune into it?"

For me, getting the Burren is about the limestone. You could classify yourself - like if you like the Burren, you're stone mad. My totally outlandish theory is that since the limestone is made up of sea creatures and it was an ancient seabed down at the Azores and then moved here - well my own view is that we are evolved from the sea - there's something that attracts us all to sea and to water. I think that's where we came from. My own weird theory with absolutely no evidence is that within the limestone with all those sea creatures there's the origins of where we came from. That, I think, is what grounds me here.

The other part I love is the flora and fauna and the beauty of the plants and flowers that grow and the mixture of them growing together. Like yesterday we saw some beautiful gentians up on the hill there and I was even saying "What we should all do is join hands and sing 'The Hills are Alive with the Sound of Music' and run down." There's that feeling about it. That's really what the Burren is for me.

I love the beauty of the gentians - the colour. I remember looking for them for years and never being able to find them and seeing other bluey flowers and wondering "Is that them?" Yet when you see one you know "That's it!" Something hits you and maybe it's the beauty of it - there's probably something in the colour - the deep blue and the fragility of it.

I find sometimes on the walks with the walking club it can be more like a hike - you're going along to get from A to B. I know we're with a group, but I'd prefer at times to be on my own and stop and take it in. Like when we went to Machu Picchu last year we got to the hotel and did a tour and the next day we were going to climb some other peak nearby which had a greater view and I just said "I don't want to do that - I just want to get a little bit high up and sit and take it in." And that's what I like to do here. So it's great doing the hikes in terms of exercise and it does help your head, but I'd much prefer to stop along the way and look around and take it in. And maybe go off track a little bit.

There is something about going down into the shaded areas and that - on some of the tracks it's all moss and the trees are coming in over you and you see your insignificance and sense the nature around you more. It's a funny sensation - like I sometimes get if I'm driving along a very narrow dark road at night with the headlights on - like going through a tunnel. I can't explain it but it's like you sense the smallness of you in some ways surrounded by whatever is outside of that. But it's also lovely like up here when you go to the wall at the top and go to the right - there's a natural amphitheater up there. And it just sits down in the valley. To me, it's one of the most beautiful places in the world just to sit down there and look.

Again there's something about the Burren - because it's been inhabited for so long and there's all this so there's a sense of life all the time. And I've always been interested more in how people lived rather than the history of this battle and that fighting so and so. For me, I'd be more about how people lived and their lifestyle. And also the people who live here today and them talking about the old ways - Mick Carrucan and people like that. So what I'd sense from some of those stories is that they'd real hardship and tough, tough times. I remember Mick telling me about back when a packet of cigarettes was only a few pence and one guy was looking to borrow half a penny to put towards a pack and for the whole week, nobody he met had it.

To me there's a simple lifestyle around here which gave people more - happiness isn't the right word but contentment or satisfaction with what they had. Mick told me another story about an uncle of his that lived in Fanore and he had never travelled anywhere until one day he got the opportunity to go to Galway and when he came back, he said it was the best place in the world.

Veronica used to live next door here and she's a photographer. She did all the fantastic photographs in McNeill's pub of the old characters. She told us she was going to do something on May eve - she wrapped the Poulnabrone dolmen in saffron-coloured material - the colour of monk's robes. So she wrapped it up that night. I thought it was a great idea - a great statement about gift wrapping the Burren as if

Image courtesy of Veronica Nicholson

it were a commodity. And people were disgusted because the tourists came - the buses - and they were disgusted about this thing and local people were annoyed about it as well. It was only wrapped for a couple of days because the reaction wasn't good overall because people come here to see the dolmen. But their idea of coming to see it was they just wanted to come and take a photograph and move on. That's why I thought it was really good the way she did it.

So when we went up, the first ones we met there was a family with kids and the kids were saying "Oh, what happened here?" I said, "You know, this is the time the fairies come out and maybe they did it." And the parents were like "Oh don't be saying that! They'll ask loads of questions now." But I love the idea - you know on May eve they tie a bit of gorse to the door and that used to be done to keep the fairies away because they're travelling at that time and that stops them from coming up to the house and doing mischief. It's the same with Halloween where there's the idea of spirits moving from one world to the next. A lot of the old Celtic thinking would be that it's very easy to move from one world to the other - to the point that if I owe you money, I can pay you in this life or the next because the lives are so interchangeable.

I don't know if Veronica did it for the fairie part of it or if it was deliberate that it happened May eve. But when I went back to the gate, I saw this elderly woman who was disgusted. I acted innocent and asked, "What happened here?" "Oh," she said, "There's witches over in Gleninagh! Witches!!" And she was going to go in and burn it. I said, "You'd probably do more harm than good." "Oh!" she answered, "You're right - I'll just sprinkle holy water on it instead."

It would probably be unfair to keep the Burren as it is - things are always going to change - but my dream is to see people visiting and physically spending more time getting out and about in it. Like, I say, the buses annoy me - picking people up in Dublin in the morning, driving them past the house here, stopping at the pinnacle well and telling some yarn, then on to another site, take a photograph then back on the bus to Dublin. I'd like to see people really experience it; get out and walk and see it. But obviously, they would be people who appreciate it rather than just to take the photograph. My fear is that the Wild Atlantic Way will get it overrun. And I've noticed that - even one thing that's happened is what we call 'the sat nav generation'. For instance, if you put into the sat nav to go from here to Lisdoonvarna - it directs you up Cappanabhaile because that's the shortest way distance wise. So now we're getting traffic going on minor roads purely to get from A to B and these are roads that have grass growing up the middle. That's ruining it for the people who like to walk there.

My fear would be it gets overrun and I think that's something with Ireland as well - We rejoice that there's now 10 million people visiting Ireland. If you're in a business obviously you want it to grow. And if that grows at 10% every year - 10 million will become 11 million and 11 million will be 12.1. So in 7 years, it will be double. 20 million in 7 years, 40 million in 14 years and 80 million in 21 years which is total madness.

The world, the way it's constructed, is based on growth. So if you're starting any business whatever you're doing it has to grow otherwise nobody will invest in it or whatever. But the growth is totally unsustainable. For example, if you take a lake and let's say 12.5% of it is covered in weeds today you don't really notice it that much. But if that doubles that's 25% weeds then you say "Oh, there's something going on here." Then the next day there's 50% and, after that, it's totally covered. So we have this idea of growth.

On the other side of it, growth has brought an awful lot of benefits to the world - it's a sad statistic but more people die of obesity than die of hunger in the world. There's a Swedish guy - Hans Roling who died recently who did a Ted Talk I saw online, and he talks positively about growth and he said: "Things have improved in terms of people dying of diseases. "Like we've eliminated polio. So in the last 100 years, we've done a huge amount of great things. And I couldn't believe this but the average mortality rate in the whole world is 70.

So anyway, growth has brought lots of benefits but the whole idea really is a con because something has to give - you can't keep doubling every 7 years in what you're doing. We have to get to a stage where we're not growing but we're sustaining and we're keeping going. That, I suppose, is what I'd like to see here.

We laugh about the Finn McCoole myths and fairie stories or some people do. But today the one myth that all of us believe - and it's the biggest myth and the biggest con job - is that money; the 10 euros in your pocket will buy you a lunch and all it is a piece of paper. But as long as I believe it and you believe it this myth will take off.

Paddy Bogside in Derry used to say something like "Imagine you're on a ship and, say for the sake of argument, there's 5,000 people on it that reflect all aspects of humanity. And this ship is sinking with only one lifeboat and there's a deserted island far off in the horizon and you know if you get there you'll survive. So who would you put in your lifeboat? The people that we adore and admire and talk about forever - most of them you wouldn't put in. Like are you going to put in a film star that's paid huge money or whatever? You'd probably put in a farmer, you'd put in an engineer and a doctor - people who could sustain life. But the people that we seem to spend most of our time looking at, admiring, adoring and chasing are the ones you wouldn't put in the boat.

Elenore Quigley
Sea Swimmer and 2019 Unofficial Mayor of New Quay

A friend of mine once went for an ordinary, routine check-up to find out if she could have open heart surgery – absolutely risky, frightening surgery. When she came out, she said the only thing she could think of was getting back in the sea. About months later she was back in swimming with us and is still at it. Everyone who swims here has said how amazing it is. In the morning everyone's tired but it wakes us up. Kay who started up the swimming group with me four years ago likes to talk about how invigorating it is. And it's infectious; people that walk on the shore have started waving to us and some even join in.

What I love most of all is the prayer circle. It's not religious but we make a circle and send positive energy to anyone who needs it. Everyone is included in the circle; lapsed Catholics, Catholics, Quakers, Methodists, Church of Ireland. There's something to me about a circle 'cos nobody's in charge. It started one day when we were in the water talking about a friend of ours who was very ill – we just decided to pray for them then and there – it was very organic.

There's nobody in charge of the group but when I organised an evening swim people started questioning me if maybe I was putting people in danger because the water was cold. My answer was "Shure, everybody's responsible for themselves." And during the storms when we got in after being told to stay out of the water, fair enough, I did start to think "Should I be sending these text messages out?" And then I'd argue with myself that I'm dealing with adults after all. But still you have to think of the responsibility – like if I sent a text out and then three people drowned – that's what makes you think.

It was dreadful during the storm around Christmas time when we were all told to stay out of the water. But one thing that came from all those storms is that I now understand the pack mentality. I see now how teenagers get into trouble because when we get into a pack, we all do the same thing. And even though the stones were moving under our feet, flying past us, we were in hysterics laughing; it was pure dangerous, but you get a high from it and when you came out you felt amazing. But in fairness on those days I did send out texts saying, 'Red alert warning issued.'

Kathleen after a dip

In the winter I would stay in for 15 minutes. We don't seem to feel the cold anymore. I would love to see the whole brown fat thing you are supposed to get from swimming being researched in depth. Why are we not feeling the cold? Like, is it from our brain? Are we born with this brown fat, or do we develop it unknown to ourselves? I'd love to know. Kay was missing from the swim for three weeks once because she was sick and when she came back, she said the pain from the cold of the water was unbelievable; she was like an older person with rheumatism but then she was fine again.

We swam during the snow last year. I thought to myself before getting in "This is going to be hard." If you shout it helps; somebody did that in the water one day; a big "A-A-A-A-A-A-G-G-H" and it definitely serves a purpose. Sometimes when we swim there are hailstones, they're like free acupuncture to me *[laughs]*. And being able to stay in the water at stare back at the Burren when it was snowing was fabulous.

When I'm in the water it feels so beautiful; you could just leave me there. My mind goes totally empty; nothing crosses it, no worries, absolutely nothing. The time my husband Bernard was waiting for his kidney transplant, I honestly believe that coming down here is what kept me going. And the prayers in the circle made me believe that we would make it. Like Kay often says you can go into the water in bad form, but you'll always come out happy. And we have great chats in the water. Some people swim and others, like me do a little joggy uppy and joggy downy. Like we might talk about what went on in the book club last night or how people are doing and it's great. You know, I nearly think that if meetings from the Dáil and all these places were held in the sea they might talk a lot better and have far more positive results. The water is a great leveler and it makes your mind clearer. And the fact that they'd all be in their swim suits and no one would look fancier than anyone else. I'd love if someone started up something like that.

I do believe that swimming here at Flaggy is an addiction. I adore Dublin – I grew up there and used to think nowhere was outside the Pale. Nowadays I go up to see my Dublin friends but when I'm there I'm thinking "Oh, I'll miss the swim on Monday, I'll miss the swim on Tuesday." The cove we have here is so special. I think it's the feeling that it envelops us that attracts me. I've been to beaches where it feels more open and feel a little fearful there. Fear is something that can destroy us. Some people get scared of the jelly fish here in the summer and it's not nice having them but as I keep saying they were here before us and they have the right to be here. They own the ocean and we only share it with them.

We have a seal who comes to watch us here sometimes and I love him. He is starting to come nearer these days. One day you could even see his whiskers. Pauline was right beside him when he appeared, and she screamed – maybe it was because she was wearing a black swimming cap and he thought it was a friend *[laughs]*. He had such big eyes. We call him Friday because he's been coming since Good Friday four years ago. It's funny – he looks at us as if to say, "It's those ones again *[laughs]*".

There are 68 in our whats app group now and it's easy that way because Kay and I just send out a message to say what time the swim will be on and you might get 2, 4, 6, 16 or, in the summer, 26 turning up. There's no pressure to it and it's irrelevant how much or little you swim. And we do different little things like during the solstice we did the nicest thing – I know we shouldn't – but we lit a little fire in the rocks, and we all sat around having a barbeque at 5am. It was beautiful the way the

Prayer circle at Flaggy Shore

sunrise lit up the water. I'd love to have a dawn and a dusk swim. In the summer we have evening swims and we do our best to work around the tides, but the morning swim is usually around 9 and often we have to walk for ages to get to the water's edge. And we make fun and say "Guys, now you have to do the lap of honour!" And we're colder than cold.

Some people say we're up the wall doing this, but the majority of people think it's wonderful. My son-in-law is a rugby player; he's muscle throughout and strong. One day he joined us here for a swim and he nearly took pneumonia but, in our group, we have two asthmatics who have never had an attack since joining the group. I had to take early retirement because I had chronic obstructive pulmonary disease, but I haven't had one chest infection since I started swimming the sea every day. And in our prayer, we ask for four things for ourselves; to be protected mentally, physically, emotionally and spiritually. I think these four things are so important – I'm totally convinced in the power of them together.

And the swims get us out of bed in the mornings. It would be easy to lie in bed if you had nowhere to go but you know the others will be joining you so that motivates you. Sometimes I might have a late night and think I'll go back to bed after the swim, but I come home so energised and usually just heading straight for the bike and do the loop cycle of flaggy; it's just so beautiful here.

And the amazing thing about this area is the cost of living. You'd spend in one day in Dublin what you spend in a month here. And here you have real beauty. I'm bored with clothes shops now; bored – totally bored. Also, you get so healthy from the sea you are not spending money on medications. Of course, you sometimes need medicine, but I think it would be good if more people could try this. In our group we have people from the age of six to way past retirement and I see so much benefit in them. And it changes people mentally, they become more positive and their attitudes towards others change. Small groups sometimes can be toxic, but we include everyone here and make sure they feel welcome – the ocean is for all of us. We have the most beautiful atmosphere here with the mermaids and the mermen and I want nothing to destroy that. We're every one of us fragile; we may not appear it but we're all human. Fragile, full of imperfections and gorgeous with it *[laughs]*".

The Burren is special. There's something in those rocks, there's something in the people, I think. In Clare they love their Irish, their music and they don't mind their accents. And I love that; they're proud of who they are. When we retired here people were so welcoming. Us living up that road and taking their land but they were still so nice. And I don't care if people say, "You paid for the land." So, what?! They still welcomed us into the community. As for the place itself, I think there's something sacred here; like the rocks hold energy. We don't know the half of it. I just get up every day and look out the window and think "I have everything." As far as I'm concerned living in the Burren is utopia. My friend Kay also retired here but her Mum was local and so her best and happiest childhood memories are of New Quay.

After the swim

I also love the wells here. When Bernard was on the kidney transplant list we had to wait and wait and wait and he was just getting weaker and weaker. One day I took a scissors and cut a ribbon from his

142

underpants and tied it to one of the trees at St Brigid's well in Liscannor. Three weeks after that we got a call and he got his transplant and he's never been better. And the ribbon is still hanging there on a little bush inside the grounds of the well. I do believe that some places have to be spiritual and it doesn't matter want denomination the people who go there are – they are all praying, and they bring a lovely light and calmness. I love the feeling at that place and I'd certainly tell anyone to go there.

Rosemary Power
Burren and Iona Pilgrimage Leader,
Author & Academic

In 2008 I was asked to come to
County Clare and take on a job with the
Methodist church for 5 years to see if
pilgrimage could be redeveloped in the area as a kind of ecumenical Christian activity. As part of this, we had several development groups some of which walked the routes which lay mainly between ancient sites. We would stop at each place to speak, often to pray and certainly to sing.

We had a pilgrimage that took us to Kilfenora but the main places were in mid-Clare, in the far west around Loop Head and the holy wells. There was another one through East Clare; along the Lough Derg site like Holy Island. Different groups would follow at different times; some were complex to get in and out of. The people who came on the tours were hugely mixed. Most had been contacted by the churches, some, particularly overseas visitors, turned up by chance. We had everything from Bishops to Druids; they seemed to get on together and what seemed to work was the mixture of historical input and an understanding of the sites and also the stories that had accrued about the saints engaged in the sites and ways of interpreting these using poetry but particularly using music either to listen to or to sing to - the singing bringing people who normally didn't sing together. This happened mostly along the stopping places.

Most of the pilgrimages were to do with the process of walking and what that loosens up in people who walk either together or alone and whether it helped people to do things they did not normally do like the singing. It was also to do with the reactions of the local community, like, in one place a local farmer joined us and, at the end, brought a stone he had carved on a stone carving course and we used that in our final ceremony.

The only opposition to what we were doing actually came by email from Americans and was occasionally abusive, particularly as this was a Protestant-led project. What they were getting at was that we were invading Catholic territory and we were trying to colonise it. I would often bite my tongue because I thought "Well actually as a taxpayer I am also one of the people contributing to it." I have to admit on one occasion I did just write back in Irish and this seems to have ended the conversation [laughs]. But on occasion, they just wanted to be abusive about Protestants.

There were two reasons that the church wanted to explore pilgrim paths; one was that in the 2006 census they found an astonishingly high number of people in Co. Clare that identified as Methodist or Presbyterian - there were 700 when the usual number had been 30. It appears that most of them were African and left Ireland during the recession; they had contracts here but when the contracts ran out, they left or else they had joined a local black-majority church; we simply don't know; it was one of those strange blips but part of my job was to administer to the congregation in Shannon which was largely black.

The other reason is that, on the whole, they were very conscious that the pilgrimage thing had been taking off; The Compostela route was enormously popular and demonstrated a thirst for the spiritual in people, part of which was the notion of walking and walking together and in the modern context you could walk a chunk of a pilgrimage one year, fly back to work and do the next chunk another year. Obviously, some people do it all in one go but they might be retired or for some other reason have the time that a medieval person would have been able to take. So this was a chance for people to connect with the Celtic tiger and offer something that was gentle and across the board and open to people exploring the spiritual. At this stage it was 2008 and nobody realised the crash would come. But, in practice, most of the Africans did not come partly because they had no interest in the ancient aspect that we covered in the pilgrimages and also because many were involved in such manual jobs that they were on their feet all day and the idea of walking on their day off was too much.

But the two dynamics were there together; it was an exploration of the home mission to offer something in a role that would give without expectation of return.

The project finished early as we ran out of money due to the recession but I still lead pilgrimages. I haven't done this so much recently in Clare because most of my work is on Iona in Scotland but I hope to come back here to redevelop it.

We did the Christianity very light as not everybody felt completely comfortable with it but we were quite specific that this was our drive. And we also tried to avoid some of the ultra-evangelical approaches which are not intended to be insulting but if you go around claiming 'Clare for Christ' this can be very offensive to local mass-goers. So, it's about softening down and being respectful as we were walking through land which not only was owned and farmed but was also precious to people. And it was important to respect that preciousness while also enjoying it.

We found, sadly, that whilst we were initiating this quite a few other groups did so in a competitive rather than collaborative way. This included another one of the Protestant churches which made it quite difficult to find sufficient space. And, further, there was one person leading spiritual walks of the Burren as his business and we didn't want to in any way disrupt his life.

I think it is important to have collaboration rather than competition. Shortly after writing a booklet on Kilfenora, I discovered another group, completely unknown, who had set up a whole display in the cathedral and were doing their own thing. They did this with a certain degree of research which would pass reasonable historical muster but which might have been stronger if placed together with other groups. And then there are the ethics of who does what and how do you conjoin and are you actually serving the local people by being in competition and is any of this of relevance to them.

So, there are possibilities there but it's all about how you do it. We had hoped a bit of microbusiness would evolve in the stopping places and were also encouraging the notion that the people who stop do not necessarily need Bord Fáilte B&B style with fluffy carpets and personalised soaps; for them it's more about somewhere to dry their clothes, get a solid meal for the evening and possibly breakfast and a pack of sandwiches. Hostels are better equipped in that regard. We also found that for those groups who did stay together of an evening the group discussion of the past day was a crucial aspect of the pilgrimage walk.

Whilst researching Kilfenora, we heard that at one stage in the 18th Century both parts of the cathedral were still roofed; the choir end was used as the Catholic church and school and the nave end was used as the Protestant church and school with a dividing wall between the two. That would have been quite common in early times, not to keep one side out but because when churches downsize or can't maintain a whole cathedral, they very often do this to make each part smaller and warmer; especially if there is a declining population. That seemed to have gone quite harmoniously but it was probably technically in Church of Ireland care and control at the time and was also a cathedral with a dean who lived about two miles away.

We know about the dean because of an account in which one of the crosses was stolen. Well, maybe not quite stolen but in the story the dean of the time wanted to impress his new bishop and said that once standing crosses lay on the ground. This meant the locals had no interest in them so he got out a horse and cart and took the cross to Killaloe and put it up as a feature in his garden. Subsequently, it blew down a couple of times and then in the 30's was moved into Killaloe cathedral. So we might imagine that, possibly, relationships became less harmonious and the Catholics ceased to worship there. I don't know why but possibly they were even able to build their own church. At that stage, the Protestant side was refurbished and various features, like a triple pulpit, were put in. There is a bit at the back where the poor could sit and, delightfully, this is around the hearth. There are three hearths in Kilfenora, one in the vestry, one for the clergyman at the front and one at the back for the poor; this is still functioning and the space is useful.

In the 1800's, Kilfenora became increasingly poor because the railway didn't come there. Up to then it had been this great centre of the cattle mart where the cattle who were in calf came off the Burren at the end of winter - and that had made it a great place of selling and suchlike but with the railway going elsewhere it became less significant.

Academics and others can help us to look at the levels below the superficial story and this can enable people's imaginations to take off so they can do their own relishing and experience rather than having to listen to someone else's interpretation. One of the benefits of academia is that it helps us unpick the stories and particularly the lives of - say - the local saints because there are layers which we may not immediately understand; we may only understand the top story level. The danger of the modern Celtic spirituality movement has been to take that top-level literally and then try and reinterpret it in their own terms for today and often with a very narrow interpretation - sometimes one that sticks. But this is sometimes done without the academic understanding that underneath the top level are a lot of suppositions or aspects that would have been known to the original audience. For example, one of the stories about Saint Columba is that when he knew guests were coming, he would grind the grain to make the bread or the porridge to welcome them with. That was traditionally such tough work; turning quernstones was the work of slave women - the people at the bottom of the pile - and as an aristocratic man and churchman he was reversing that entirely. These are the kind of things we need to know. Columba also was visited from Ireland by a crane and this isn't just a pretty story about him telling his monks to go out and look after this crane until she gets better and can fly on; cranes, which were plentiful in Ireland at that time before they vanished in the 17th Century, are ultimately associated with St Columba and are almost like his milieu. It's my belief that in one of the carvings at Iona Abbey it's St Columba's crane that you see distracting the devil; he's on your side whilst your good and bad deeds are being weighed at your hour of death. So, if we think it's just an animal story, we miss the significance of the other crane stories about Columba and that this was possibly a message from his own people.

My personal view is that Kilfenora has an enormous sanctisimus vellum around it. Cattle would come down from the Burren in winter in calf, so if you're a monastic centre and you want manuscripts, well the best manuscript comes from a newborn and it's best to do everything on site. That's not just imagination because from where I stay in Sutherland, I look across to Portmahomack which had a monastery burned by the Vikings in about the year 800. And there, archaeologists excavated every process from the slaughter pens through the making of vellum with lime bath - and there was plenty of lime at Kilfenora from the limestone - into the scraping, the stretching and finally the cutting and the writing; the whole process was happening in one area.

And if that was a common process you could see how Kilfenora had a large significance in earlier times and was chosen in the 12th century for this very large cathedral which appears to have been at the end of a pilgrim route through the Burren and around which the round tower and other places could be developed.

One of the pilgrim routes seems to have been skirting the lower Burren and Peter Harbison has written on this. There were openings at Rath and Dystert O'Dea coming through Kilnaboy which seems to have been a very significant site. All of these had round towers which would have been great marking points rising above the skyline. Peter Harbison has interpreted the high crosses in Kilfenora as being the end of the pilgrimage.

Local pilgrimages would be done quite often, maybe once a year on a particular day and these seem to have very ancient roots. On the whole this is folk tradition so we can't trace it back before the 18th Century but throughout the middle ages we know there was a great desire to travel and pilgrimage to the major international sites like Compostela from which you either went from St James quay in Dublin which is now otherwise occupied [laughs] or from Dingle.

Some people pilgrimaged by boat and we have records of that going way back to the royal pilgrimages of 9th Century Ireland. I think historically it is difficult to say what the shorter pilgrimages were about because there is much more written about the longer pilgrimages and certainly John Wycliffe of 14th Century England detested them, especially for women as they were an opportunity for fraud, debauchery, lechery and other misconduct. It was something people prepared for; they often made their will and sorted out their business because they may never come back and you had to have quite a lot of money to do it. But also, for some people, it was definitely the package holiday. And even a relatively local pilgrimage could have that element because in 19th Century accounts there were large amounts of drinking and dancing on your pilgrimage and on Patrons day, as well as stories of young men trying to steal young women. And so there was obviously quite a lot of rowdyism which is why it was stopped. But I think the deeper level is the desire and the yearning to meet yourself and your God and find yourself on the route. This is one of the great dynamics of pilgrimage and I think that's true today even if people don't express it as such.

And now pilgrimages can have a kind of sideways relationship with the development of public walks and leisure. Sometimes they coincide with traditional routes and sometimes, as in Co. Waterford there is a move to try and preserve what was a medieval route and give it protected status. There are practical issues here whereby the walk route would use bridges where the medieval route ends with a river and I presume you would have used a ferry. But this relates to the need to protect and preserve ancient routes and possibly reuse it in an environmentally friendly way so it doesn't damage any archaeology.

I think the difficulty with the Burren is making sure that the footfall is sustainable. And whilst also accepting that it is the right of everybody to explore their spirituality and enjoy ancient sites but also understand them. Signage can be difficult because a local interpretation and an academic or management one do not always coincide but there needs to be some way in which they can be joined so you have cohesion. Because, obviously, that which is believed locally has its own validity and also that is how it has been used - as long as the information comes from an ethically-sound local source.

The difficulty with signage is also something that we find on Iona. There's almost a desperation within the heritage industry to make these secular and, quite bluntly, consumable; that people are there to consume an experience to which they are directed. I mean, signs can be rather secular in a sometimes-jovial way. But quite often people are not there to consume, they are there to have their own experience and any signage which assists them in doing so is useful but it's not the experience and it's there possibly just as an underpinning to enhance. So there is also another level of sensitivity between preservation, which is the duty of the state bodies, and acceptance that these are spiritual sites and people have experiences here that can't be encapsulated on billboarding. And so there needs to be an acceptance for those who are out walking for enjoyment that for others it is an intense time of spiritual exploration. We need to be sure we're not tone deaf to certain levels between the formal conservation level and the respect for local people to the enjoyment of walks.

But the walking itself - the journeying -is often as important as the arrival and sometimes the going back can have an impact, even after the pilgrimage is finished. Like, if you go somewhere as a pilgrim there are different stages; there is the process of going, the being and then the return to the place where you come from. And different people have their moment of spirituality at different stages during that process.

So yes, I think pilgrimage answers a very deep, innate urge

in people but how we interpret it is very delicate. And there are remnants of life in the Burren that far predate Christianity and how do you incorporate those? It would be stupid to ignore them because they are there on the route taken.

I think one of the benefits of pilgrimage to everyone is that somehow if you go with some experience of prayer or communication with the divine, although you probably are not aware of it, you are leaving that into the atmosphere as well as receiving from it. And so when you pass to somewhere else, you leave that behind. I used to offer services in Kilfenora before which I would pray alone not knowing if anyone would come and it was very much as if the whole cathedral was reawakening from a kind of deep sleep. Once we had a German group in there and you could feel afterward the resonance; it was almost if the building was enjoying the fact they had passed through and had their enjoyment.

On a personal level in Kilfenora I am struck by the layer upon layer of knowledge that this has been a holy place. I find it quite different an atmosphere to sit in Kilfenora - granted it has a roof - and to sit in Kilnaboy. And whether that's down to the Catholic-Protestant thing or the fact that Kilnaboy was used as a church into the 18th Century - it was thatched apparently at that stage - I don't know. But each place has a different kind of atmosphere. And Kilnaboy, I would say, is a place of deep healing. This is somehow something I gain in the atmosphere there and possibly I'm reacting to the sense of deep feminine in the place though we don't know anything except that it's named after a female saint. We don't know if it has a female foundation and it was later a parish church. I have no views on whether Iníon Buí actually existed, you know, and it could be just a place name by which girls who wanted to be nuns could go and therefore they were daughters of a concept.

I'm open on the issue of ley lines. I can accept the original walkways between different sites; that sounds extremely practical and sensible. And they are not only visual points of contact but are quite often on high ground and you'd want to walk them. I haven't had any particular reason to think about them on the Burren by themselves but I have had a couple of experiences which would make me feel that - certain points would give you a sudden burst of some kind of energy which is like an electric bolt but does you no damage. I don't know what that is any more than why some people can water divine and some people can't.

None of that can be put easily into academic terms but I believe that academia should notice that this is how a significant number of people experience places. Somehow, we have to leave a record of these things which are beyond research but nevertheless real to a wide range of people. It's to do with the relationship with the divine which lasts forever - and this is the sort of wild element that makes pilgrimage so attractive.

Finavarra

CHAPTER 5
FROM THE OUTSIDE IN

Protecting our Protector

What did this land and its network of underground springs mean to the monks? Were the nutritious crops that came up through the earth, graced by the sun just a means of survival? In an era when famine was normal, they didn't have a lot of food coming in. Some may have travelled, via the pilgrim trails from Jerusalem, through Italy and France but it was limited in supply. And so, they needed the land, they needed the water, they needed the rain, they needed the sunshine; they couldn't have lived without all of these things. And with the recent experience of drought in Ireland, at a time when countries across the 1st world remember what it is to have food and water restricted, maybe we can begin to understand the lives of our medieval ancestors.

"*Barony of Burren, in the county of Clare, famous for Physical Herbs the best in Ireland, and equall to the best of England. Here are Eringo Roots in great quantity. Oysters of middle syze, salt, green finn'd, farr exceeding our Colchester, as own'd by several Judges of both; this Barony affordeth not a piece of timber sufficient to hang a man, water in any one place to drown a man, or earth enough in any part to bury him. This consists of one entire rock with here and there a little surface of Earth, which raiseth earlier Beef and Mutton, though they allow no hay, than any land in this Kingdome, & much sweeter by reason of the sweet herbs intermixed and distributed every where.*"

From Cromwellian Officer
Ludlow's 1651 Memoirs

Eringo (Sea Holly)
growing wild at Bishops Quarter Beach

Patsy Linnane
Farmer from Ballyvaughan

I'm that kind of man that was always into the sky and the stars and all that kind of stuff. I had an interest in the technology too but in my time, there was nothing like that. And there was no work or only primitive work and that's why most people had to emigrate and many of them so talented. We had that de Valera leading our country then; he puts us back 50 years. It vexes me when I think of it you know because the Irish people were talented; we had the art of thinking and that's lost now.

It was a hard life in those days but we still appreciated it. We just had a gas cooker for the cooking. The day we would kill the pigs we'd put on the fire and boil the water. You always reared two pigs together because they thrived better. And then you sold one and you bought one so you always had two little ones and every six weeks you had a new pig in the barn. My mother was very good with the fowl - we kept ducks you know. We kept hens too - there was a special chick you bought in those days for killing; they were called leg horns; they fattened very fast. My mother would've sold a lot of eggs that time and we also sold potatoes. We had our own beetroot, our own lettuce and our own carrots parsnips and turnips. We'd milk a cow or two and kept goats so we were kind of self-sufficient in that department.

We had our own special separator to separate the milk and then you'd get the butter in a churn. My mother was a very meticulous woman; everything had to be spotlessly clean. Everybody knew that and so everything would be right She wouldn't just say it would be alright; everything would have to be properly done.

I must admit that we were always busy; we were like the bees because there was so much to be done. You had to be in the garden and then the hay would have to be cut. It wasn't like it is now but we had the mowing machine. Then the tractor came in and you would hire fellas to do it; it was very labour-intensive. When the winters came, you'd have to feed the cows and you'd be cutting the hay with the hay knife. And you had to feed them fodder. We were always working but I didn't know any other way. That's how it always was; we would have to go to the bog to cut the turf and it would be very hard if the weather was bad and you'd have a lot of weeding to do in the garden. You wouldn't have had the sprays like you do now although I think the sprays are bad.

A lot of the cows were going up the mountains in November. Sometimes a cow would have a calf up there and there might be a problem and you'd have to carry the calf down. In those days the fertiliser would come in a cloth bag and I'd put the calf into it, put it over my shoulders and walk down the mountain - it was tough but you didn't realise that. People would come back from different countries and say that over there they have things like combine harvester making bales.

You had to come back to the Burren to appreciate it. I always say to people "Heaven is all around you if you can just see it." I moved to Dublin when I was 18. I had to witness it. It was a big change but something I had to do because rural Ireland well… you have to get out of it. They spoil you in the city; you have the doctor, the hospital and the dentist - everything is down the street. And in the city, you can just go round the corner and there's a shop. It can be a more convenient life. In Dublin they had hard times too; there were a lot of poor families in the 70s because the country was not developed. Now you have the rich people. But that's okay too because if you don't have people with money, they won't develop the industries or whatever.

I'd get two weeks holidays from working on the buildings in July or August and come home to help my father with the hay. When my father died in the '80s I came home to live. My mother wanted to transfer the farm over to me - I never asked for this - but the solicitor wouldn't let her because he'd seen too many people put into the nursing homes by their children after they got the inheritance. The place was neglected by then because my mother had been sick; she had cancer. They have better ways of treating it now but they didn't then so there was an awful lot of work in it.

Before Ireland joined the European Economic Community, the land was what it was and you did what you did and didn't do what you couldn't. But that all changed; there was a kind of farming plan with the European system. You'd go to Teagsc and there was a particular man appointed to deal with you and he'd come out and advise what to do with the place and the animals. You can have all the advices you like but you still had to be born and bred into the Burren to farm it; the people of the Burren had the understanding of the land and how to work with the hills.

One time in the 70s, I was on the way to work and saw the front page of the Irish Independent. They said they were going to close off the Burren and have hardly any people in it or houses; they just wanted to have tourists drive through it. And then there were all these rules and regulations and the only outsider that came around and listened to the people was Brendan Dunford. He never showed his hand; he just wanted all the knowledge and I shared it with him. I feel it's fools wisdom if you die and the knowledge goes with you. He used to go round with a bag on his back; he was like a student. Then we got the literature about the specialist conservation areas; the SACs coming in.

When I laid the farm road up behind the house there was a revolution. I said to Brendan Dunford how short-sighted the people in authority were. They don't have to carry a calf down the mountain in winter. I did the road as far as the well first because I was limited in funds. All my land is SACs (Special Areas of Conservation) and NHAs (Natural Heritage Areas). And when the NHA thing was about to come in I had to finish the road to the top of the mountain quick but the weather was snow and hail and rain. I don't regret any of that because if you don't have PMA (positive mental attitude) you've nothing and as the Indians said, "You must never look back."

I remember my mother used to say to me "Always sleep on something - let it keep to the morning." She was right. Sometimes you don't appreciate those people till they're gone. If you get nasty about

something you've blown it. Diplomacy is a great philosophy - never release the safety valve when you are mad at someone because if you release the safety valve, you'll say something you might regret.

A lot of research has been done on my land and the big advantage of that is they found out that the four most important chemicals; selenium, cobalt, copper and magnesium are missing. And they're very important for the human not alone the animal. You can tell by a cow if she's lacking in copper because her hair will be dry And she'll never take the bull because if you're lacking in copper you never become pregnant - it's an awful important element you know. In the winter I leave the licks out for them but then in January and February they would be following you and telling you they need something else. So I'd get that Burren feed or something for them. And I get in the oats. You can't beat the oats; it would make a horse run or a hen lay. You get a fit calf when he's born from the oats; he's hardy, slim and trim - not a big fat slob; they're nearly up on their legs in a heartbeat. That's where science and natural farming methods work well together.

We are different in the Burren to the rest of the world because we put all our animals to the hills for the winter. And for every day there they have a fresh bite of grass, they never have to lie in the same place twice, they're sheltered from all the prevailing winds and they have natural water. But the most important thing is they have the heat because you have 800m of rock in the Burren and that takes the heat all summer. That's why the top is warmer than the bottom for them and they love it. So what you have is a fit cow not a fat cow and with that you've no problem calving.

What I'd explain to you about a cow - and it can happen with the woman too - is that if the baby is coming wrong and she was inside in the shed or slatted house you have to call out the vet. But if she's up the mountain she'll lie down and she'll turn over and turn again because she knows she can move around to shift the calf inside her. But if she's kept in the shed or a slatted house, she'll forget that. This's what a lot of people don't realise; they're reading books but they're not coming from the nature. If the nature didn't have its own solutions there'd be no animals; they'd all be dead. But it's very important that you have a fit cow on the mountain and that she'd be moving every day. And it's very important that she has all the minerals.

Pajo is the name of my bull and he's very healthy. The first time I put Pajo up on the mountain he was very aggravated and was like "Where am I going?!" The cows were there but he couldn't see them, then when he did, he was happy. The first thing then was he saw another bull at the neighbour's wall and he roared into him to let him know "Don't come in here! This is it now!!" Some people don't put their bull to the top of the mountain for the winter but that's where he wants to be. And he minds the calves; a bull is very protective of the calves. A cow or a bull will stay with the calves while the mothers have their feed.

Pajo makes up his own mind about when he comes back down. One day he was waiting for me at the well and he wanted to come down even though the cows were still up there because he knew he would be

Patsy with his beloved Pajo

treated well at home. He has put on weight since he came down last but he's not a big slob; he's healthy, muscular and glossy.

It's against the nature of an animal to be inside; they love it up there because it's always clean for them. We always wash and clean the troughs before they go up for the winter and I do everything I can for them; I make sure everything is above board. And I cut the ends of their tails cos then they're cleaner and look smarter. And it helps to tell your cattle from the others on the mountain.

There's an energy at the top of the mountain and even people who go up there walking find it's good for them. If you watch for the cattle you will find they lie where there's high energy and the calves know it too. They love it down by the wall; there's a very good energy there and they can shelter from the prevailing winds. They lie down at night in a kind of a circle and the heat builds up among them. There's a massive heat coming from animals; you'd never think it unless you were inside a shed. In a shed they'd probably sweat too much unless it was very well ventilated.

But the animals get very dirty in a lot of sheds. A man came one day and said to me "Is this the first time you've used your pen?" and I said "No, I always wash and disinfect it when I'm finished." and he said, "That's why you're clear of disease."

You inherit intelligence, you acquire education, and common sense is not much to have but a lot to be short of. Many people around here - you can't get through to them. If you were telling them things they'd say, "That fellow has gone for the birds." But I'm not; I'm very well-tuned in to the animal kingdom you know. Pajo gets so offended if you don't recognise him. So all you have to do is stop and say, "What a fine man you are." I was telling people this on the mountain the other day and they were laughing at me. I said, "You're perfectly entitled to laugh but I'm genuine." Like he feels so good when he's recognised. You have important people in all walks of life; you have politicians, you have educators, you have doctors and they deserve to be recognised.

Like I said to my medical specialist in Limerick - I said, "You go to school for one third of your life and then people come here and probably don't listen to what you have to say. They hear you but they don't heed you." So, I said "If they do what you tell them they would have a chance." Pajo is top of the herd - you must have good cows in every farm but if you don't have a good bull you don't have good offspring - so he's half the herd 'cos if you don't have good stock you don't get the money afterwards.

If you respect the bull, he won't touch you. Pajo is used to walkers going up the hill. I just tell them that you have to recognise him. It's amazing the amount of farmers that don't know that. One man from Galway told me about a bull that's treated terrible - he is beaten into the pen and he's prodded with the fork. I mean, jail he should get for that because a bull will respect you if you respect him; it's like people. And one man came to do his hoofs and he said to me "Is he wicked?" "Oh no" I said, "Very cultured man this fellah." And we get him out and he just went along with what we wanted him to do.

Note: Sadly, since this interview, Pajo had an accident and after the best possible care met a humane end. He will be fondly remembered for decades to come by ramblers the width and breadth of the Burren. Patsy's land is now overseen by the proud and well-cared-for Pajo II.

Harry Jeunken
Farmer from Kilnaboy via Holland

Nature wants to heal and nature really asks people to connect. That's why we are here on the planet earth; we really have to assist. To know what we have to do we really need the ability to find out where we should step in and where we should withhold. Otherwise, we might do more damage. It's lucky for me that, as a farmer, I have been so close to nature and to living processes that sometimes you know that you have to stop because something is not going well. On the other side, you see "Wow! That was good what I did. I have to continue it."

I bring school groups around the farm here but I never studied myself. That's lucky because if I studied in modern universities or colleges, I might not get a clue. But it's important to have brains and also good body; we need both. So in any day, people should have some physical work and, of course, you also do the brainy stuff. Because that's the beauty, that's where animals won't come in. The monkeys are quite near but animals do not have such a complete brain set as the human beings.

So, yeah, use the brain and the body to look after places. It depends what job you have; if you have a farm make sure you keep doing things manually when you can and introduce only a machine if it is not possible or if it is not harmful and use it sensibly. That's what we do here at Lough Avalla; we do a things lot manually because it's better; you stay in touch with what you're doing. With a machine it's different; you have a lot of noise and weight, it has a lot of power and might be dangerous, it might be harmful for the soil because it compresses it and the worms will be squeezed. A machine can do damage far more than human beings but we can do damage even without the machine. Nowadays for the slightest little thing, they invent another little machine, a new gadget or electric thing for the house or whatever and that's the industry. They are making so many things and, of course, it's nice but technique is important.

Wheat and certainly soya have high protein but a complete protein needs 14 amino acids in it. Wheat only has eight or nine amino

Harry's Belted Galloways

acids, soya has eleven or twelve. But the good protein in fish or an egg or the good milk - milk from cows who eat mainly grass - those proteins are often superior. When we have school children here, I tell them about the egg. If you put a fertilised egg in an incubator at 40 degrees or under the hen for 24 days then out of nothing - no connection with the naval - grows a live chick. And that's the indicator that the protein in an egg is so complete that something living can come about. So I tell the children, "If you are vegetarian that's OK but please eat eggs - excellent protein. And if you're only eating the plant-based ingredients eat the good protein."

When I bought this farm in the 80's I had to find out why there's so much rock and even in the rocky areas so much division of fields. The reason farmers made fields on the rocky bits in the Burren, as well as the meadows, is they wanted to rotate animals even in the winter; they had winterage blocks you see. That is the beauty in Ireland - Scotland has more big fields - but here in the Burren and maybe Donegal you have many, many fields with all these walls that were built so long ago. It makes sense to have a walled enclosure because, for example, in a walled garden the plants will grow better. A stone wall in a circle or square or rectangle can keep an aura; an energy. So it is always good that you make fields and surround them with either a wall or whitethorn hedge. The whitethorn hedge has almost the same ability as a stone wall to keep an energy. The whitethorn is a sacred tree in Ireland; the fairy tree. And that is what you had in old Ireland; the hedgerows and the stone walls. Much of it is gone now around Dublin with the big fields so we lost a lot of that heritage - that old setting and now they have to compensate for this with artificial fertiliser. But you cannot rely on the fertilisers because you need good habitat for the plants, animals, insects and bees and then for human beings as well.

I learned by following the sheep, cattle and goats; you see how they behave. And then every night I have to take certain books and study - to read about what we might have seen; to find out about the real connection and how it's working and how that functions. That's why it's so nice to be a farmer; all your life you're learning and every year is different. That makes you not want to retire - to stay and see where the process goes, where we can improve or discover things.

I learned also from seeing other farms because if you see a lot you learn things. Like many people who follow the walking trails around the farm here come to me and say, "I have seen so many things today, I cannot list them but I will go home and note down the things I have seen."

When I came here, the place was completely neglected; you couldn't walk to the well and the green meadows were all encroached with hazel and blackthorn so you couldn't see the potential to make a living from it. I had to just start from scratch by making fields again like they did on the Aran Islands, introducing animals and knowing which animals to introduce. In Ireland the cow was already here; everybody spoke about cattle and then they had a few sheep, a few goats, a few pigs. A cow will graze different from goats, sheep or horses; a cow eats with the tongue - she pulls up the grass whereas a horse, goat or sheep will bite the grass. When you have too many sheep in a meadow they can, with their nose work selectively through the grasses to take out a herb. The cow never can do that; she has to take the whole lot with her if she wants to take a herb. But because she uses the tongue, she hardly can take the root out. She takes the long grasses and leaves the fertility. That's why you need cows in the system; they keep much better flora.

It's important to study about eco-systems; study about what energies certain plants, trees or animals can give and study about soil health. Plants need minerals to keep them healthy. So, if disease strikes you need to find out what's missing in your soil because nearly all diseases can be cured by the proper nutrition. There's always clostridium in the soil which causes blackleg and that's normal. I remember when I came here and they said: "You need to inject for blackleg." Sometimes I might inject if the cattle needed something but I don't for everything.

For example, TB is a problem in Ireland but there's no TB in Denmark, in Holland, it's not in Belgium, not in Germany, not in Switzerland - none at all. It's thought to be in Ireland, Scotland and Wales and maybe, in France. A TB outbreak can come about only when you have a deficiency in your grass, in your silage, in your fields and when four minerals are missing. These are copper, zinc, cobalt, and iodine. If those four minerals are on a good level, it seems that TB will never strike. And TB is not contagious; in Ireland, they say that if a cow gets TB you will have to kill the other cows in the herd. But it all depends completely on the immune system if TB comes. If there is something missing in their diet only then can TB creep in. And if a cow is sick with TB and you adjust their diet then TB can be phased out in the body. You just need to find out which minerals are missing from the land, lay them out on the grass where the animals will eat and they will become so strong again.

The deep-rooted plants often can draw up the coppers in the subsoil but if the grass is continuously fed with artificial nitrogen compound fertiliser or slurry, the plants have no incentive to root deeply; they are waiting for the next dressing. And then you see those fields still have lush grass but some elements are missing and so you might suddenly have a TB outbreak. So as farmers we need to understand what minerals are important, which plants might have it and if we can draw the minerals up. And if we can't do that then we need to replenish the soil in some other way. This is what they do in Denmark, Germany, and Holland.

As well as knowing what's missing from the soil you need to make sure that land can drain itself; it's no good if you're standing in a wet field in your shorts. So make sure the animals have a dry footing and the land will be naturally drained and don't compact the soil. And then, replenish the plants on the land after erosion. Because when you harvest crops every year you take away certain minerals - you need to replenish what you take away.

Ireland is like a rock and when we have heavy rainfall the

erosion comes and all the minerals and riches go into the ditches, into streams, into rivers and the ocean. So we lose all those minerals which is a shame.

There are four things in life that are important for any person; we all need a home or our own place; it can be your kitchen, your bedroom, your house; you need your own place. Number two is we all need good food for our body physically and our brain. Number three is we all need a meaningful job that has some depth - a job where you are part of something that is growing. And number four; each one of us needs to believe in something that is bigger than ourselves. Like some people say "Oh, I can do anything! I can repair all that I have!!" In other words, "I don't need anything else." But maybe later in life when they become sick, they will think different. Then they will think "What can I grab now, what can I do?" And then they will go for better food - often organic, then they might start praying or other things. But we should try and ascend this in younger years.

People tell me that when they come in through the gate at Lough Avalla they feel something because it's so alive. The conventional farmers sometimes come here and they can't believe how much grass I have in the summer because I don't use any fertiliser. But they told me "When we enter your farm there is something different that we won't find in other places." And that's just the energy, from the care we put in.

Nowadays, in modern society, most people don't want to work. They only think about their free time. They have to go maybe six or seven hours a day, soon it will be four days a week instead of five and they hope for shorter hours. But whatever work we do, it should be enjoyable. I always tell people whatever work you do has to have an element of joy; it should not be boring or monotone. Often I have workers come to help me and I make sure they have a good time. If you allow people to have a good time and support them they work great.

With regards to healing, we need to make sure we don't harm the environment. When we use telephones and the GPS we have a signal bombarded to us to say where we have to go or where we can find this or that place. Using GPS, satellite and mobile phone unnecessarily is as dirty as all the time we are beaming out signals. When the bees and insects are going across to find their place and do their things in various locations they sometimes cannot find their way back to their hives because of all this disturbance. In the oceans, there's also a lot of disturbance from the signals and that's sometimes why the dolphins and the whales come ashore. It's funny; people still don't understand this. And why should I know? Because I probably was able to learn from the land, from living systems, from being outside instead of being in college. It's common sense; I'm no better than anyone else, I don't have more brains than anyone else but it's logic.

When we pollute the climate or change it, this will affect all of us and the land. The floods we are having and the hurricanes with the people nearly losing everything in the storms like in the Caribbean islands - that's scandalous. They didn't cause this because most of them live a very simple life. But look at the way the Americans behave, look at how China is burning so much coal to be number one in the world in producing goods. It's all about power and economics. There's a lot of greed in Ireland and that's why the nurses are not respected. There are far too many occupations where people get way too much money whilst the nurses are exhausted.

Society is still so sick and so wrong in many ways that it will be difficult to do healing processes on a personal level sometimes. The good thing is I am isolated here; I am not near dirty industries so at least I should allow the place to heal. And we are part of the ecosystem so if people come here and have a good time and feel good and go home and say "Wow!" That's important. What I want is that people experience the healing of seeing good places. The main thing is that they will notice something and then search for it. They will either come back or call me and say, "I experienced that when I visited your farm, can you explain what you've done because of what I've felt?" The main thing for us is that you notice something. Like that's what happens with the people who go in the planes, they don't notice the energy that's needed to run them and that's very bad. A plane is a good invention but use it wisely.

So, there are a lot of forces outside of me that put a dampener on what we are trying to do. The thing is to find the middle way where you are not depressed and find things that are good and that's where hu-

Feeding the sheep

171

man-kind can support each other so beautifully. Young people are likely to be more aware of certain wrongdoings in our society; of the state of our climate and the state of our planet. Hopefully, they will embark on the right moves and do something really good about it but we have a long way to go; we lost a lot of beauty and goodness and it's hard to get it back.

One of my daughters is finishing her Masters in Soil Science but she works hard on the farm because she loves it so much. My other daughter is training to be a veterinarian nurse and she likes it very much. She has been minding all the animals on the farm here and she brings a lot of practical experience into her classroom. If ever you are a veterinarian you are fed by the multi-national pharmaceutical companies and cannot always go your own way unless you are very strong and might risk your job. One of my sons is doing a Masters in Ecology and Forestry in Germany and he's involved in the Burren Life conservation project. It's lucky that he's involved with practical work whilst studying at the university. Our youngest studied Horticulture and Nurseries and now he's a bit of an entrepreneur; he's busy with all sorts of things; he's building beehives, he has a few stalls in markets and he grows vegetables. So all of my children love nature and that's good. They like this place and that's enough - they will keep it going but it's not easy. Young people think they know so much and they say, "Oh no, I know it myself and I don't need help." But that's OK; that's the way to learn.

The start of a cosy evening

Gordon D'Arcy

Artist, Writer and Environmentalist from Belfast and the Burren Lowlands

We were a fairly big family - there were 5 kids and I used to throw my schoolbag in when I came home on a Friday evening and wouldn't be seen 'til teatime. And the next morning I'd go out after breakfast and wouldn't be seen again till teatime. My mother just knew I was looking after myself - that I was sensible enough and was doing what I enjoyed and if I got hurt badly I'd come back to the house. Getting stuck in the mud and hitchhiking and stuff like that you learn very quickly about your boundaries - what's safe and what's not. I reckon one of the reasons I'm an adventurous spirit is because my mother allowed us to do that. I think I first laid eyes on the Burren across the bay from Galway city - I saw the low profile of it and recognised it as a very strange looking landscape and definitely a place to be explored.

When I first came here I'd say I was in my 20's. I was hitchhiking and staying in a tent. And I remember coming to Carron - We were inside in Cassidy's pub - Robert's father Bobby was running it then, it was a much smaller premises than it is now. I remember sitting by the fire drinking pints and so on and it was lashing rain outside. Bobby was very kind - he put us up and didn't charge us for breakfast the next morning and sent us on our way. I was just mesmerised by the place, the people and the hospitality I experienced here. I thought it was just wonderful. Particularly coming from the North of Ireland where there was rampant hostility at the time.

When Esther Mary and I got married we decided to move west. I just said to her "Let's go live in the Burren" and she said, "Let's do it." We initially wanted to live in Ballyvaughan but were turned down for planning and then we opened our options and looked down this road at the edge of the Burren, met the owner and fell in love with the place. That was '84 and we're here ever since.

When I was a kid, I remember the teacher in school mentioning birds and how they flew and how they have hollow bones and I was intrigued by this idea of hollow bones. At a later stage, as a fellow of 9 or 10, I was a member of the Ulster Society for the Protection of Birds and people used to call to the house and take me on field trips 'cos they could see I was an enthusiast. We'd go to Lough Neagh and all sorts of places like that and I got more and more interested in bird watching as time went on. At school I did articles for the school magazine; I've still got one of them - which I wrote in 1961, would you believe, 500 words with little drawings of the birds of Belfast Lough. So that's what started me in presenting and sharing the enthusiasm with others.

Any time I went anywhere on holiday I wanted to do bird-watching and birds always intrigued me. I used to be very surprised that everyone wasn't interested in them. I thought they were something that would have caught everyone's imagination but apparently not. It's interesting that people see them as peripheral at the corner of their eye and not as something intriguing. And I suppose I became interested in the natural world through birds. Birds started me looking at landscapes and habitats and at other things like insects and mammals and the whole package, so I developed a strong perspective for conservation through birds. Everything seemed to come into focus through them.

Some people do hate bird calls - like crows or herons make loud squawking noises and people get upset about that. But I'm kind of musical and can sing and I suppose having a musical ear would help me to get into that. I'd advise people to get hold of recordings from Birdwatch Ireland - some of them are notated like you can hear someone saying, "This is a reed warbler and here is a sedge warbler" and you can differentiate between them and listen over again. But some recordings are a cacophony of sound like garden birds all singing together.

It tends to be the plainer birds who make the most beautiful song. A nightingale who tends to be known as the most beautiful songster is a very dull-looking bird - a brown job or LBJ as they call them - that hides away in the middle of the bush. Having said that, a dunnock, one of our common birds is dull looking as well but his song isn't much to listen to - so it isn't really consistent. But you could say that our really brightly coloured birds often aren't good singers. The bullfinch is a very poor singer, the jay makes a squawk, the kingfisher just makes a whistle and the wren, that's a dull little bird, makes a big long song. So maybe it's a compensatory thing with them.

What is a bird song for? It's to attract a female and declare territory; it's a statement. But a call is communication. It's important to differentiate between those two things and remember it's the male bird that sings. A lot of people think all birds sing and that it's a sign they're happy but in fact, it's the male bird that sings to attract a female and declare his territory.

The Burren attracts a lot of cuckoos because it's open territory and there are certain types of birds that the cuckoo predates - or lays his eggs in the nests of - that live in the Burren. Birds like meadow pipit in particular - a little streaky brown bird that lives in open country where there are no trees - it squawks when it flies up in the air. Also, skylarks, dunnocks and occasionally robins but robins are well able to look after themselves - they are feisty little birds so they tend to steer clear of trouble because that's the way the cuckoos operate - they're sneaky.

And that's why the cuckoo goes to the Burren; 'cos they're able to get on top of a thorn bush, cuckoo around the place, attract a female and then the female can suss out where all the nests are that it can predate.

Other open-country birds like stonechats and wheatears, the

white throat - a little warbler that comes in the summertime - swallows and certain birds of prey like kestrels and sparrow hawks also do well in the Burren. Long-distance views are possible as there are no big buildings or high trees; it's a place that you can get a handle on quite quickly if you're a bird that flies high or who needs a high perch to see distance as there are escarpments everywhere.

The Burren has never been better protected than it is now - it's really enjoying a great time of conservation particularly through Brendan Dunford's efforts in farming for conservation; the Burren Beo project which has 170 farmers involved. This is the process of letting nature express itself - not using fertiliser to any degree, trying to protect watercourses and the quality of water - all that's part of keeping the habitat right. But the Burren's inclined to go back to being a forest and because farming is diminishing and families are moving away from family farming and the scrub is encroaching it's turning back to woodland so the question is how to work that in favour of birds or nature in general. It will create a different habitat which will be enriched by certain species but it will diminish the grassland where you get lots of flowers. So open country birds are going to become less favoured and maybe the cuckoo will decline. Birds like goldcrests, tits, warblers and bullfinches thrive on scrub.

The black cap has increased since the 1980s, the little egret, the collared dove, the Mediterranean gull - those are all birds who have come up - this might be due to climate change - and colonised this country within the last 10-20 years. It could well be that the black cap is part of that movement. It is difficult to be sure about it - you really need to look at these changes in terms of long passages of time. It'll be necessary for someone to look at this in 10/20 years' time and say, "Is that really what happened?" But I remember going up to the woods below Cavehill in Belfast to hear the 1st black caps that had been heard in Northern Ireland. That was so rare 40 years ago and since then they're in every wood so there's been a massive incursion of them.

The encroachment of hazel scrub is a recent thing. I can notice massive differences since I came here. There was a lot more open country in the '80's than there is now. But I'm quite happy with the way things are going here.

The problem is a broad ecological problem really - it's hard to get the farmers to go along with the overview that a conservationist would have.

I believe we should have a natural browser like red deer in the Burren eating the hazel. The red deer were there until about 1600 and were preyed on by wolves. But the two of them were eliminated very quickly in the 17th Century when the Gaelic system collapsed and the colonial system came in; the Colonials wouldn't tolerate the wolves and the deer were very quickly eliminated with the new attitudes and intolerance that came with that whole regime.

So, what you've got then in the Burren is a sort-of-depleted, out-of-kilter ecosystem which goats are having to do the job in. Now there's no predator controlling the goats apart from man and that would

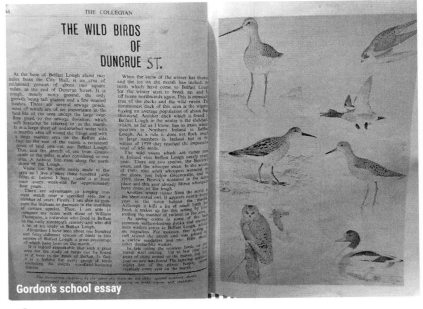

Gordon's school essay

be the way if the deer were brought back because there's no way you would bring wolves back into the Burren unless you had some way of kraaling them. So, the thing of how the Burren would be in the future is a tricky one cos you've got to win over support for the idea of there being a natural browser. And deer are going to get back into the Burren anyway no matter what happens - You're not going to be able to stop them from getting in because they're in East Clare, in Tipperary and adjoining counties but you don't want those deer to come back because they're fallow deer - they were introduced by the Normans. I think the native red deer should be brought in here and if and when they get out of control they should be culled and the venison sold as a natural product from the Burren - I think that would be a great thing to do. Someone has to grasp the nettle to do this because otherwise, you're going to have to have much more management than is necessary. I mean, how are you going to control all the hazel scrub if you don't?

I don't approve of Round-Up at all and a lot of people don't. Even with selective use of herbicides, you are still going to get run off into the water table. Especially in limestone country where everything goes straight into the aquifer.

I don't believe in weeds. I take all the dandelions out of the gravel in the driveway because I want it to be pristine, it's one of the few concessions I make to gardening - everything else can do its own thing but I just want to keep that area clear because if you don't it ends up being a mishmash of things. For me, dandelions are a wild plant in the wrong place but I'd still never call them a weed. When I work with schools I do a lot of drawing with the children and one of the plants I draw is a dandelion to show them just how beautiful it actually is, You know, it has several different developmental phases; when it first comes up it's like a flask with a little tuft on top and then it bursts open and you get the yellow flower and then when it goes to seed, it develops into a globe which you can blow - like a clock and after that goes you end up with a kind of button on top of the stem. So we draw this and the famous dent-de-lion leaves and then we go out and look at the actual flower. And it changes attitudes - when people go out and look at something like that in terms of its particularity they tend not to see it as being a nuisance. Instead, they see it as being something that - OK it's very common - but that doesn't diminish its beauty and its uniqueness. It's the same with any plant; if you look closely you'll see that it's got a particularity of form that is interesting. It may not conform to the conventions of garish beauty like a rose or an azalea but it'll have its own particular characteristics that are interesting and unique. I think that everything's intrinsically beautiful - maybe beauty is the wrong word - we use this word for all sorts of things - but intrinsically interesting - we'll have to invent a new word for that particular thing. But I do believe that when children look at something closely... like we found one of these ground beetles yesterday, it ran across my hand and we had a good look at it and you could see all these little bits and pieces - the six legs and the little antennae with kind of frills on the top and when you turn it over it's bright violet underneath. All the children I was with were intrigued by this and how you can turn it back over and put it down again - and those are kids who might have stood on an insect if they saw it walking across the path. They won't stand on it after seeing it like that. That's the thing I'm trying to get across; everything has its particular beauty and interest.

In the chain of things, nettles are useful for butterflies, Butterflies lay their eggs on nettles and when the nettle goes to seed birds will feed on the seed. Our garden turns into a seed factory. All the docks get their rusty-coloured top, the bullfinches move down on those, goldfinches come in after the thistles, so it becomes

Heron at Loughraslc

a menagerie because of the way we leave it. It's not manicured or cultivated in any way – it's just let go its own way. We have planted native trees but they just produce things like berries on the rowan or acorn on the oak.

I get a lot of wellbeing from nature - I just like seeing the seasonal changes. I like seeing the 1st leaves on the trees. My wife Esther Mary is the same - she will say "The spindle's got its first leaves" or "The oak is late this year" or whatever. So, we do take note of the vegetation and how it connects with the seasons or how the seasons connect with it. And in the winter time we're pretty safe from the storms because we have the trees around us and that gives us a certain buffering from them.

But when it comes to dealing with children relating to nature - a lot of them might know about the Amazon jungle or the Serengeti but they might not know about what's happening on their doorstep; like how to pick a blackberry. That's a pity because it suggests a gradual removal away from the natural world. That's connected to the obesity crisis as well as stress and strain amongst teenagers culminating in suicide and other psychological problems.

Over the last 20-30 years the percentage of the world's population living in cities has gone up to 60%. And so, a lot of people don't seem to need the stuff that I need. I came from a city - I was reared in a city but I don't feel comfortable in a city. When I'm in a city for a weekend I want to get out of it again - it's long enough for me. But OK, that could be eccentricity and I'm quite happy if it is. It may just boil down to personal attitudes rather than a general human characteristic but I'm unapologetic in this. As far as I'm concerned, the natural world is where I want to be. I don't even know whether you can put that into words - a lot of what I do is inspired by the natural world and that inspiration is manifested in painting and illustration and writing but it's also evident in peace of mind, in there being some sort of structure to the world and connection to the non-human world. Those kinds of things are meaningful to me. I suppose if I trawled my brain for long enough, I would come up with other reasons but those are fairly good ones as far as I'm concerned. I actually feel as if I can connect with a divinity or the totality of things not necessarily in a moral sense like a human moral sense of good and bad and so on but in a sense of gifted-ness. I kind of think that the planet and everything in it is a gift - I see it that way and I'm grateful to experience it. And I put great store on giving in human terms as well. I think that's one of the great character-istics of humanity - the capacity to give, whether to one another or to the planet. Does that make any sense?

It's all quite hard to define in words and I'm not worried about that because it's like art; art lies on the periphery of things and it's often between disciplines as well. Art emerges from that kind of interface so I think it's good to muse over these things but not necessarily try and define them or hold them down with words you know, because I think words are always inadequate.

CONCLUSION

The Burren, a place where St John's Wort, a well-known cure for depression, and an array of curative herbs grow wild is seen by many as somewhere where people come to heal. For over 100 years, its stillness, clean bays and pure air have replenished weary travellers taking respite from intense city lives and the bright smiles and wit of its people often warm the hearts of those who pause to stop and shoot the breeze.

Since moving here, I've joined three all-year round swimming groups and have the choice of georgeous, seaweed-nutrient rich, if chilly waters to bathe in early each morning. Local hill walking groups keep many of us villagers busy in the evenings and at weekends. The mental and physical benefits of changing to a life where shared joy take precedence over racing out to buy the latest device – though technology can be a wonder too – have been huge. But obviously, you don't need to live in the Burren to experience these gifts. Nature, love and joy are all around us. The people who've inspired and contributed to this book share the message that it's the small offerings of magic that count. If once in your day you see a flower growing through a crack in the concrete, a child smiling, or a break in the clouds letting in a corner of blue sky then you've felt it too. If we eat foods that are natural and good, find a means of connecting with something bigger, whatever name we give it, and exercise our bodies, love, forgive and find clean air to breathe then we are allowing ourselves to be nurtured by nature.

BIOGRAPHIES

 **Eilís Haden-Storrie** (editor and photographer) has worked for over 20 years as a researcher, production assistant, writer and educator in broadcast and print media. Eilís trained with RTE and freelanced on shows such as 'Ear To The Ground' and 'Glenroe' but most of her work has been in Northern Ireland where she worked with various bodies including BBC News and Education and ran a small media organisation which produced European Union-funded films and publications for museums, councils, schools and peace organisations. Eilís grew up in the Burren, a place very close to her heart.

 Eamon Ward (photographer), a Clare man whose father comes from the Burren, has won numerous Irish and international awards the most recent being Irish Press Photographer of the Year, 2017. Eamon freelances on a regular basis with The London Times, The Observer and The Irish Examiner.

BIBLIOGRAPHY

Printed Sources

David E. Allen & Gabrielle Hatfield, Medicinal Plants in Folk Tradition, (London: Timber Press) 2004.

Gordon D'Arcy, The Breathing Burren, (Cork: The Collins Press) 2016.

Alick Bartholomew, Hidden Nature – The Startling Insights of Viktor Schauberger, (Edinburgh: Floris Books) 2012.

Anne Byrne; Ricca Edmondson, Ricca; Tony Varley.

Introduction to the Third Edition of Arensberg and Kimball and Anthropological Research in Ireland (Ennis: Clare Local Studies Project) 2001.

Thomas Cahill, How The Irish Saved Civilization, (New York: Anchor Books) 1996.

Paul Clements, Burren Country – Travels through an Irish limestone landscape, (Cork: The Collins Press) 2011.

P.J. Curtis, The Music of Ghosts (Kilnaboy: Author) 2003.

Dr Eamon Doyle, Dr Ronán Hennessy, Dr Maria McNamara & Zena Hoctor, Stone, Water and Ice (Ennistymon: Clare County Council) 2017.

Barbara F. Harvey Monastic Dress in the Middle Ages – Precept and Practice, (Canterbury: Chapter Library of Canterbury Cathedral) 1988.

Michael Houlihan, The Sacred Trees of County Clare (Castleisland: Author) 2016.

Michael Houlihan, The Holy Wells of County Clare (Castleisland: Author) 2015.

Carleton Jones, The Burren and the Aran Islands: Exploring the Archaeology (Cork: The Collins Press) 2004.

Cecily Kelleher & Anne MacFarlane, Concepts of illness causation and attitudes to health care among older people in the Republic of Ireland (Galway: National University of Ireland, Galway) 2002.

Malcolm MacLachlan (ed.), Cultivating Health: Cultural Perspectives on Promoting Health (New Jersey: Wiley) 2000.

Anne Murphy & Cecily Kelleher, Contemporary Health Practices in the Burren (London: The Irish Journal of Psychology) 1995.

E. Charles Nelson and Roger A. Stalley, Medieval Naturalism and the Botanical Carvings at Corcomroe Abbey (County Clare).

(Chicago: The University of Chicago Press on behalf of the International Center of Medieval Art) 1989.

John O'Donohue, Four Elements: Reflections on Nature, (New York: Harmony) 2011.

Rosemary Power, The Celtic Quest – A Contemporary Spirituality, (Dublin: The Columba Press) 2010.

Tonja Reichley, Wild Irish Roots – A Seasonal Guidebook of Herbs, Ritual and Connection (Denver: Author) 2017.

Brendan Smith (ed.) The Cambridge History of Ireland, Volume I, (Cambridge: Cambridge University Press) 2018.

David Steindl-Rast, May Cause Happiness: A Gratitude Journal from the Teachings of Brother David Steindl-Rast (Louisville: Sounds True Inc) 2018.

Wolf D. Storl, The Untold History of Healing – Plant Lore and Medicinal Magic from the Stone Age to Present (Vermont: North Atlantic Books) 2017.

Matthew Stout, Early Medieval Ireland 431-1169, (Dublin: Wordwell) 2017.

T.J. Westropp, Folklore of Clare (Ennis: CLASP Press) 2003.

Essential Websites

Professor Arne Björnberg, Health Consumer Powerhouse Ltd, Euro-Health Consumer Index Report 2017, https://healthpowerhouse.com/media/EHCI-2017/EHCI-2017-report.pdf

The Burren Centre, http://www.theburrencentre.ie/the-burren/

Stephen Daniels, Lines of Sight: Alfred Watkins, Photography and Topography in Early Twentieth-Century Britain, Tate Papers, no.6, Autumn 2006, https://www.tate.org.uk/research/publications/tate-papers/06/lines-of-sight-alfred-watkins-photography-and-topography-in-early-twentieth-century-britain

Dublin City University, The National Folklore Schools' Collection, https://www.duchas.ie/en/cbes

Cyril Ó Céirín, A Handbook to Lisdoonvarna and its Vicinity: An Introdution, 1998, http://www.clarelibrary.ie/eolas/library/local-studies/clasp/publications/lisdoonvarna_vicinity_introduction.htm

Dr Gerard Mansfield, Dr Claire Collins, Ms Ivana Pericin, Mr James Larkin & Mr Fintan Foy, Is the face of Irish general practice changing? Irish College of General Practitioners https://www.icgp.ie/go/library/icgp_publications

Houses of the Oireachtas, Sláintecare Report, https://www.oireachtas.ie/en/committees/32/future-of-healthcare/

Fergal Lang - harvesting oysters